Anonymous

The rival captains

Hastings-onia Ramble-tonia

Anonymous

The rival captains
Hastings-onia Ramble-tonia

ISBN/EAN: 9783337153083

Printed in Europe, USA, Canada, Australia, Japan

Cover: Foto ©Andreas Hilbeck / pixelio.de

More available books at **www.hansebooks.com**

THE RIVAL CAPTAINS;

OR,

HASTINGS-ONIA, RAMBLE-TONIA.

PUBLISHED BY E. W. ALLEN,

11, Ave Maria Lane, and Stationers' Hall Court,

AND TO BE HAD OF ALL BOOKSELLERS,

AND AT ALL BOOKSTALLS.

1879.

ERRATA.

Page 18.—On 9th line—read " Arabesque " for " Arab-sesque."

,, 123.—Read 7th line thus—" Yet Cupid has a Rival —Passion."

" 133.—On 1st line—for " Monkry " read " Monkery."

,, 144.—On 18th line substitute an adverb for the pronoun.

,, 187.—Read 18th line thus—" God knows for best not, lets things go amiss."

,, 200.—10th line, capital A for Absolution.

,, 220.—10th line, capital S for Scotch.

TO THE READER.

HAVING once inadvertently published a book without a preface, sad fault was found by friends thereat. Profiting thereby (as I had hoped), in the next a preface was inserted. The same before-mentioned (how grateful all ought to feel blessed with such!) then said, "A book should need none." Ever wishing to please, I am puzzled what to do this time. Bearing in mind the fruitless labours of, in that line, a certain old gentleman, immortalized by Æsop, who possessed a donkey, I will allow the above-mentioned to call this an either or neither, which they please. Can I be more obliging?

Next to wishing to please, my next desire is not to offend. Referring to the two chapters touching on Sectarianism—nothing, I need add, is intended *individually*. Whether or no I have written too freely (not, however, as forcibly as I perhaps may) I must leave each reader to judge. But that some strong remarks are required in This Present Age of Rival Religious Trickery I feel convinced. That they are out of place in so light a work as the present may or may not be. But volumes could not better illustrate my intentions than the last compound sentence of the following extract from a leader of the *Daily Telegraph* of a few weeks back, and with which I now conclude :—

" Whatever we may think of the tone and purpose of the free thought prevalent around us, it is neither 'cynical' nor 'low.' It indicts old creeds on the highest moral grounds, and breathes an intense desire for the elevation of humanity."

Hoping that my satire may not offend, that my lighter portions may please, and that my more serious touches may be most carefully weighed before condemned,

I remain,

Yours truly,

THE AUTHOR.

HASTINGS-ONIA RAMBLE-TONIA

OR

THE RIVAL CAPTAINS.

Flashing Lightning Speed—The Mainspring of Thought!
And of Action Muscular!—Where lie they?
The last than the first, more bewildering —both
Spontaneous! curbable! improvable!
The former setting in motion the latter,
How—none can say, nor by what; some calling it
The Soul—that mysterious life essence
That knows nor definition nor meaning;
A subtle substance, more subtle than thought,
Yet the progenitor being thereof
As indefinable by its offspring,
As though it progenitor never had;

Thought being, in manner, progenitor
Of Action ; that, in turn, neither knowing
By what subtle power setting in motion
Mechanism, profound inexplicable !
Deeds resulting, ever developing ;
Life making wonderful ; Death making more so ;
For of what avail this fathomless all ?
Thought but making to revolve, yet ever
But returning to from whence it started.

— — — — — — — — — —

— — — — — — — — — —

Grew man spontaneous, like Action, Thought,
Ever developing more perfectly ?
And, if so, for what grand final purpose ?
Thereon (later) to bear God's gift, keen reason bring :
Without, hearsay knowledge is a dangerous thing.

PREFATORY.

Critics Poesy, Mark The Title Page!
And ye Sophists Subtle! of The Age,
To Chapter Ten! then kindly turn,
There Author's Self-Opinion learn,—
" Pray laugh not, I am no Poet,
A Rhymster Poor, and I know it."
Nor,* to be, does Ambition Prompt, for*
Artists with Artists ever war.
And covertly sneer jealously,
Ay, much more than zealously.
But it is best they should,
Otherwise, art would
Degenerate.

* * The author is perfectly well aware that this is condemned by
some. He could have easily altered it, but prefers it to remain.
having intentionally so written to prepare for the gradual break in
the metre.

Yet of late
Prompted
Said

Sore,
What more
Is left for
Ambitious Wight
Upon which to write ?
Exhausted are Tales quite,
On Love Subjects —in that line,
Nothing New presents to define ;
Ev'n to Rhymsters nought is left, they say,
New to write, except in an odd quaint way
Queer metre invent ! What age it is,
Writers' brains to set in a whiz !
How to cater for tastes all
Puzzles scribes, great and small ;
Tales are overdone,
Laurels all won,
Long ago.
Yes, Oh !
Woe !

Then,

If when

I began,

Scribes had outran

All grand subjects quite

(Age of exhaustive light)

Mercy extend, pity give

Misfortune in such Age to live.

Aim shall I, therefore, but to amuse,

Should you, patient reader, deign to peruse.

Yet, lest this new metre, rhythm, measure,

Should afford you nought of pleasure.

Gradually will I drop

A syllable, then stop;

Lest Poets should rave,

And say I crave

For glory!

Stor—y?

Wee.

Yes!

I guess!

(As they say,

In their quaint way

The Yankees) not much

Is left for writers such

As poor I.   Let me not rail

However, at Destiny—Tale

Commence, or rather, "Introduction."*

---

   * Believing this style of metre to be thoroughly original, the author takes the liberty of christening the same "The Diminuendo Crescendo Jokeylorum." Should anybody, however, feel inspired to attempt enlarging thereupon, there is no reason why "the Crescendo" should not be extendedly syllableized "a mile or two."   But "The Diminuendo" must ever remain the "sublime same" unless writers indulge in "silly-syllabical-fractions."

INTRODUCTORY.

Wet days are most wretched by the "sea-side,"
For what can be done to stem rolling tide
Of the blues, which over most men then creep,
Except to play billiards, or go to sleep?
Hotels ought to have such books as amuse
Visitors subject on wet days to blues;
Though of what books would not readers complain,
When suffering from blues and seaside rain?
On such days, it seems, at the best hotel,
An age ere the waiter answers the bell,
Who looks, when he does, as much as to say,
"What on earth do you want in my way, pray?"
In such a rude, surly, sulky manner,
Creating desire to hit or hammer
With poker, fire-shovel, fender. or tongs,
This man for imagined insolent wrongs;

Or worse deed do, to drive off the feeling,

Of black blue devils over you stealing.

You order, perhaps, a pint of sherry,

Hoping the same will make you more merry :

But more than top heavy must you well be

To counteract wet days by the wet sea.

Oh ! wretched ! wretched ! is constant mizzle,

Most discouraging, is sea side drizzle.

For wet damps the sole, makes heart feel to be

About the size of the heart of a flea—

Highly grand study anatomical

For learned Doctor Serio-Comical.

Ladies with needle work much better fare,

Non-failing amusement everywhere ;

Than men they indoor confinement less mind,

Possessed of patience, they seldom fault find ;

Than men ! most women are sweet angels pure,

Who smile at a life men would not endure ;

As proof, men's pastimes with women's compare—

See ! women have few—the men largest share—

A walk, a drive, and a look at a shop,

And most ladies' pastimes come to full stop ;

Of outdoor amusement 'midst human life,

The husband has most, the least has the wife—

Of tennis and archery clubs there are

A sorrowful few too scattered by far—

But of these and all they possess, men share,

Men may—but not women—go anywhere.

Yes, women through life have worst bargain got,

Domineering and selfish are men, I wot.

But how comes it thus? Ladies, yielding in mind,

To men are all that is generous—kind,

And, no matter (thank heaven !) whatever their station,

Can—will—not dispense with the Lords of Creation.

In coffee-room sitting one day alone,

Listening to rain and the sad sea moan,

The papers having read through, through and through,

Until I, by heart, each word therein knew,

I rang the bell hard, and when waiter came,

Of circulating library asked the name.

(I missed my Mudie and Co., and Willing,

And Smith, where this may(?) be bought for a shilling)

" Circulating library, sir ?" said he,

" Do you mean, sir, where they lend books out free ?

There is not such an one in this whole town ;
For lending a book they charge half-a-crown."
" Half-a-crown a book ! " I said, in surprise.
" No, sir; for that you get four weeks' supplies."
" Heavens, man ! stop here a month.   Look at the rain.
Not for me, thank you ; back go I next train.
Ask your manager to lend me a book—
Stay ! (a thought struck me hard—see the mark !—look !)
Bring pens and ink, I will write one myself,
A Book of this Town, for your mantel-shelf
And drawing-room table, for all to read,
On drizzly wet days if a book they need."

I began to write, but ere I had done,
The rain ceased, and brightly out shone the sun,
Which, with effect magical, changed the scene—
Pantomime-scene-like turned blues into green,
Red, yellow, golden, made all things look bright,
That before looked dingy in the dull light.
Umbrellas by sunshades now were replaced,
Young children and nurse-girls on shingle raced,
Spades, pails, picks, shovels, and other such toys,
Were used with a will by juvenile boys,

Who strong fortress made, with tiny redoubt,
Of soft sea sand, where the tide had ebbed out.
Sailing-boats danced on the glistening wave,
Sailor-dressed-land-yachtsmen now became brave ;
Sooty-black niggers banjoed on the sands,
Mixed music was heard from subscription bands ;
Donkeys with four legs, others—hem !—with two,
Marched forth, as if they a thing or two knew ;
Fashions, ladies latest, also appeared,
As if the fair wearers no expense feared ;
And last, but not least, the Piano grinder
Ground London airs, as a Country reminder.

My waiter, who I once thought was lazy,
With marked attentions now drove me crazy.
No sunshine affected him much the same,
Past inattentions, then, harshly not blame ;
He had had blues, and so had most others,
Waiters, barmaids (sweet feminine brothers)
All ; but things now looked as clear as a bell,
Like the wine they serve at the Queen's Hotel,
Where all things are done remarkably well ;

Although boasts Hastings hotels quite as good
By the score: for be it well understood,
Impartially I this history write—
Historians always the truth quote quite—
Lest other landlords might ask me to fight.)

As sun shone forth, reigned gaiety supreme,
As with Rip Van Winkle, the Past seemed a dream.
Now Nature appeared in colours bright dressed.
In sunshine bright bathed sea sparkled its best.
Visitors gay vied in pleasures of quest,
Oh, Hastings! of seaside resorts doubly blessed
Is—ever in season—Imagine the rest.
Finally, let me proverbially say
(Enough have I written, I think, for to-day),
" Sunshine enlivens, oft drives ' Blues ' away."

Thus much having said, by way of a start,
Commence I " A Tale of a Maiden's Heart,"
Shot twice through the middle with Cupid's Dart.
Near Lover's Seat—Hastings' Romantic Part,
Shewing that after first love comes second,
Though first proves fatal, usually reckoned.

Yet bound am I tight
Thus further to write—

A sort of written bird's-eye view,
To please each Visitor anew,
With Rhymed Excursions, in and out
Of this Fair Town, and round about,
For each week day, from the Monday
To Saturday ; for the Sunday
A church list, where the preachers best,
Their hardest work, for six days' rest—
Stay, such remarks are out of place,
Ordinary life doth rhyme disgrace,
Matter of fact in prose is writ,
Yes—prose for that *is* better fit.
Then take we saunter number one,
But Ramblingly our tale will run
(Part two, Love Tale, shall be begun.)
As for Excursions round about,
Leave I each one to find them out,
On second thoughts, which are the best,
(When not as good are all the rest)
Merely will I those spots mention,
Best deserving one's attention.

PART I.

No man ever prophet was in his short
Lifetime.   Revere the living not the living :
But no sooner doth The Halo of Death
Life past surround, than lulled lessened envy
Addeth to works lustre-super, which with some
Existeth not, but only as compared
The sun's light to that reflected by the moon —
So oft doth the critic to own taste mould
(Though blessing by goading to painstaking)
The Throw of each Gambler Literary,
Past, Present, Future, all uncertain making—
Dead men's lesser words and works oft making great,
Atonement (poor) for great works, whilst living, made
 small,
And that but fluctuating capriciously.

Oh! self-immortalized mortality—Stay,

Write I, simply—in an interesting way—

That which may sell, I hope, and better pay.

    ❖   ❖   ❖   ❖   ❖

HASTINGS and ST. LEONARD'S unite,

Just where, I cannot now say quite,

But once a month, at least, they meet,

And kiss each other in the street.

Of entertainments, day and night,

There often is a little fight

Of London Artists of the First,

Nor ever have they of the Worst.

But prefer you quiet country walk,

For ramble or for loving talk,

There you can have it to perfection,

Love Walks abound in each direction,

Secluded charmingly!

                Also,

Of all places whereon to go,

Is there a Pier within this realm

That Hastings Pier cannot o'erwhelm

In beauty, grandeur, bold outline,
Yet, withal, delicately fine ?
What Scene from other can compare
Picturesquely ?

    Look yonder —There
See Castled Height, Green-Mantled Down
Grandly o'erlooking Hastings Town—
That Reminiscence of The Past,
When Saxon Harold breathed his last,
Whose Hosts before Norman's gave way,
When Reigned King William, from which day
English History underwent
A Change of Race and Government.

But not upon the Past now think,
Of the present pleasant let us drink ;
It was Ordained it should be so,
We now upon this Pier will go.

Peerless of Piers ! Sea under rolling,
Thereupon how pleasant strolling,
Or in Hall lounging ; Pavilion
Grand that could hold a small million,

Provided with accommodation

Fit for *élite* of all creation,

Wherein are bright decorations,

Flags and Banners of all Nations,

Tastefully hung, which look most gay ;

Where also oft the band doth play,

Discoursing sweetest harmonies,

Ascending heavenward to the skies ;

Whilst here and there, placed round this Hall,

Are choicest ferns, gigantic tall,

That make one think of Fairyland,

All sunshine, with its golden sand,

As we read of, in fairy tales ;

Where Nautilus, fairy-like, sails

On Mediterranean Blue,

That sea of heavenly azure hue,

Of which the poets rave about—

Fibbers awful, without a doubt.

All charmed seems life upon this Pier

Spring, summer, autumn, all the year ;

Theron Promenading *Tout-le-Monde*,

Sparkling Brunette, Bewitching Blonde,

And Blended Saxon-Norman Races,

Possessed of all the Fairest Graces,

C

Figures and Prettiest Faces
Of Womankind.

After the Sun

Earth seems to leave and day is done,
Watch yon moon rise, as from the sea,
Tipping the ripplets silvery,
Whilst wavelets ever keep on glancing,
Moonbeams reflecting, ever dancing,
Casting shadows, weirdly grotesque,
Mosaic-like and Arabseque.
Then hear the sighing surging waves,
Like zephyrs whispering in weird caves—
(Ah! weird whisperings of the wind,
How soothing to the troubled mind
Through leaves rustling—on summer sward
Reclining—Thought wandering heavenward—
Then mark the changing white-fringed beach
Of sea-foam-lace wave after each
Approaching, breaking, receding,
Nothing minding, nothing heeding,
But always moving, never still,
Obedient but to One Great Will,
Whilst sea reflects bright stars above—
Oh! who can gaze, yet ne'er feel love.

Indescribably softly steal
O'er the heart for woe or weal?

To see the glorious sun arise—
Hold ! rising sun doth few surprise ;
If I describe it, who can tell
If wrong I write or write a sell ;
Yea ! what risers late know best about
Had better be my guide throughout—
Avoiding attempting high soaring,
" Fatal facility ignoring,"
(Phrase overdone sickening boring
By idiots parrot wise-cawing)
Indulgence, True Critic, imploring

PART II.

Fame! Fame!

Fleeting Fame!   Furl

Thy Flag! for thou dost last

Timely—a moment!   Favoured they

Thy sons are, yet but fade away like flowers,

Nor live they and their works but a few hours.

What are ten thousand years?   A day

Scarcely commenced—here—past—

Whilst Wide Worlds Whirl

The Same.*

---

* Those remarks, applied to the Deminuendo Crescendo Jokey-lorum, will not apply to this new metre except in as far as syllabical extension goes.   This may be called " sich-a-gittin-up-and-down-stairs two-steps-at-a-time style," which title repeated correctly, nine times in a breath, may be called a tolerably creditable linguadental-in-and-exhalative performance.

For the benefit of those individuals who require a miscroscope with

＊　　＊　　＊　　＊　　＊

To Fairlight Glen! to Lover's Seat!

To Dripping Well!—a Scenic Treat—

Oh! who will o'er the Downs so free,

And take a six-mile walk with me?

Where the rarefied atmosphere

Is so refreshing (when quite clear),

And invigorating to inhale,

Cheeks turning crimson—once so pale—

To healthy colour, ruddy bright,

The eyes make sparkle with delight,

At Panorama seen below,

Where once the sea did overflow,

Ages—Ages—Ages—Ago ;

Where anchored shipping rode at rest,

Safe, safe from angry billows crest,

In Hastings Harbour—now no more—

Whence Sea receded by God's Law,

---

which to see an elephant, I take the liberty of pointing out that the
corresponding rhymes will be found in the first and last—the second
from the first and last, the third from the first and last, &c., lines,
until they meet in the middle.

Ages—Ages—Ages—Ago ;
Where never more the sea will flow,
Until a million years have flown,
And earth shall be thus older grown,
When others, perhaps, will see again
The sea o'erflow, where bricks contain
Now humankind, in keenest strife
For existence struggling—Such is Life !

(God help the honest, now-a-days,
To hold their own against the ways
Of the unscrupulous legion,
Who invest every region
Of this too small globe.
      Reflection,
Upon natural selection,
Convinces the theory is right.
Now, victory belongs to might—
Yes, Money—Might now wins the day,
Whilst puny right but pines away,
Leaving nought as reparation,
Save hopeful heavenly elation.)

See, on West Hill, you Castle stands
In ruins—
        (Passed through many hands
Of ownership long, long since dead,
Who, perhaps, did deeds of ill bloodshed
And many crimes in ages past,
Before they took that journey last,
To gain reward or punishment,
For lives here well or badly spent—)
A once Strong Fortress, now in decay,
Fast—Gradually—crumbling away—
Fast! Fast! Fast! when we think of Time
And Vast Eternity Sublime ;
Gradually! when we think of man,
And man's short life, what little span
It is in this World's History,
Before man learns The Mystery
Of The Hereafter!
        In Hope live.
God created, that He might give
Happiness to Man—Eternal !
There is no Region Infernal,
Except as made upon this earth
By ourselves.

Soberly, with mirth.

If we fill homes and fireside hearth,

Self-eschew, others try to please,

Heaven on Earth is made with ease.

Thus soberly in all things live,

Try happiness to all to give,

Then happy shall we be below,

To Happier Place after go,

Aye, ere disruption chemical

Shall change body ephemeral

That matter dissolve in Thin Air—

God's Poor Image (?)—Man's Constant Care.

(God created Man in His Own Image,

No farther than that God gave Man Reason,

Or implanted in man the Germ thereof ;

He, God, giving the breath of life thereto,

By creating a necessity which

Developed Thought, resulting in Reason ;

And from the moment this Germ started life,

By stern necessity's call to action,

It grew, and grows, and will for evermore ;

Nor now, with less than some grand miracle,
Could God Himself Reason Eradicate.
Thus by Reason's gift is Man all powerful—
Subjugating the rest of Creation,
In the ratio as mind increases,
And necessity, then, luxury requires—
And also collectively immortal ;
For mind liveth and progresseth ever.
From the crude germ of its first infancy,
Growth of Reason is seen by remembering
How man conforms himself to necessity,
And, gradually improves thereupon—
(For Nature adapts not to Man on earth,
But Mankind conforms itself to Nature.)—
Actually surpassing God's Handicraft,
Who now, with steed of iron, eclipses
The steed of warm flesh and blood God lent him,
Until Man should provide a substitute,
If Man so wished ; but, which takes not one atom
From God's Glory, but only adds thereto,
By making Man more insignificant,
Comparing, work for work, the works of both—
For it is only by knowledge increased
That knowledge and knowledge can be measured).

Now lightly on the soft grass walk,

And down the Down quick let us stalk,

Through the golden gilt-tipped heather,

Herald of the bright spring weather—

(At least, such the poets call it,

Truthfully, they should black-ball it,

Spring weather, in this English clime,

Is seldom seen bright or sublime),

On, on, till we reach Ecclesbourne—

1 make mistake—I find this morn

Different route this place doth lie—

No matter! onward let us hie,

And we come to—where ?

    (Here is fine chance,

Strong sermons, hobgoblin to lance,

With old bogey embellishments

Of Heaven's revengeful intents,

Of Satanical punishments,

On suggestion—where leads our path, now?)

Let us enquire, for—for somehow

I have lost the way.

    " Pray, good man,

Please tell me, for doubtless you can,

Does Ecclesbourne lie before me?"

"If you go the way you saw me
Come up that hill," he slowly said,
(For with the walk his breath had *fled*),
"You come to Glen of Ecclesbourne."

"Ecclesbourne! They told me this morn
It lay another way."

He said,
With a shake of his hoary head,
"Sir, many an one thinks he knows
Where each footpath in Hastings goes;
But, did they know what I could tell,
Where Yonder Caves lead to, but—well."

He quite abruptly here stopped short
Checked, doubtless, by some sudden thought,
And frightened looked, as if I were
A detective honest standing there,
And he had done some foul, foul crime
He wished to hide in his lifetime.

"What Caves?" I asked, for I saw none.

" On Yonder Hill, where children run,"
He, pointing, said : " Near yon lighthouse,
Looking not larger than a mouse,
A flagstaff stands sticking upright—
The former to warn ships at night
Of danger ;
          The latter to guide
To hidden Caves, grotesque inside,
The stranger ;
          Where murder and bloodshed
Hath stained these caves a bloody red !
Ay, many and many a time,
With many and many a crime."

I saw a shiver o'er him pass,
He threw himself upon the grass,
And went into a fit.
          He groaned
Turned, low muttered, and then he moaned
And mumbled just a bit.
          I listened,
Heard, and then my eyes they glistened

With deep-rooted transfixed horror,
Fully determined next morrow
To search for that ill-gotten gold,
By murder obtained, so he told,
And buried deep in earthen pot,
A princely treasure foully got.

(What thoughts upspring on princely treasures
Obtained by unjust princely measures!
Yet how oft have riches thus been got,
And, by measures such kings made, I wot.)

From broken sentences, I learned,
His hidden spoil had thus been earned—
The hidden spoil of Richard Glover,
Of Heroine Jane, The Lover;
Yes, if of flesh so very frail,
A Hero can be made for Tale
This shall be Hero Number One,
To be by Number Two outdone.

PART III.

SOMETHING GOING TO HAPPEN

A mental morbid tapping

Felt you ever the feeling

Indescribably stealing

Shadow-wise, sombre, soul-filling,

Yet with horror not thrilling ;

An indefinable blank

Like Sun seen, blood red, through dank

Clouds setting ; a creeping o'er !

A something rapping at the door

Of the soul, angry making,

Yet with all thought, painstaking,

Reasonless clinging, unceasing.

Weird, augmenting, increasing ;

Double black blues, a sort of

But Satan may have thought of,

Wicked working to exploding,

Indulged, nor mind unloading,

Yet ever goading, goading—
A day night-mare ill forboding—
Miserables Damnable.

      *   *   *   *

What Glover mumbled, who on the grass
Fainted, now follows

                    Years back repass.

" Near threescore years and ten have fled
Since my old Ma and Pa were wed—"
Speech has of late grown so refined,
One fears to write in homely kind,
Thus both words " Ma" and " Pa" are mine
" Mother" and " Father" sound not fine ;
All words not fetched now from afar,
De maurais ton considered are.
Also is wrong the tense " have fled,"
But that I quote, as this man said ;
He said it, please to bear in mind,
Visit your wrath upon his head —
T'other boys, sir—please be so kind—
" Simple and loving both were they,
Honest ! the old pair paid their way,

And proud were they, as I grew strong,

Prouder when I grew six feet long ;

How ? I suffered not from parents short,

Shot up, as shoots from such stock ought.

A fisherman was my old dad,

Such he had been from quite a lad.

A fisherman he made of me,

My bread to earn upon the sea.

We jogged along the beaten track

Of life upon our fishing smack,

As jolly as the day was long,

With pipe, and yarn, and evensong,

Amidst winds fair, amidst winds foul,

That through the rigging oft would howl

All day and night.

    When pitchy dark,

Sometimes we thought that our frail bark

Safely would not the storm outride ;

It did, thanks be to That Great Guide

Above, who spared us, know I not why,

Whilst better men He left to die,

Sailing quite near, foundering close by.

Thus passed our lives, until one day

A cask came coasting in our way.

We made for it, hove cask on board,
It in our hold we quickly stored;
It was best foreign Eau de Vie,
Waif of some wreck of reckless sea.
Whene'er thought we it cost us nought,
Oft, oft we drank, nor much else sought,
Until quite gone, and then for more,
A craving came more we wished for,
Which craving grew from bad to worse,
From thoughts we then began to curse
The King and all the Customs' Guard.
First to the skies, then down "—"Hold hard,"
I said, "Curses, ill wishes, learn,
Almost always on ill-wishers turn."
He cursed no more, but growled, "Still yet
I often long for one more wet.

One day wind and sea got up a dance
Of waves, which carried us to France,
There landed us quite high and dry,
Near to a little hostelry.
We knew not what the people said.
But, like King James, their signs we read;

When weather bated and wind fell,

To France we bade a joint farewell ;

Kept secret what we saw and guessed,

That brandy, of the very best,

Could be obtained and quickly sold

For twice its cost in English gold ;—

Blame not if we turned smugglers bold."

And now a moment let us pause,

Whilst we discuss sad errors' cause ;

First, shall we make these men go wrong-

Just as you please, in writing song—

Set the son against the father ?

Or just the reverse write, rather ?

Or virtuous heroes make them ?

Or, in chains, to prison take them ?

What mighty weapon is a pen,

In fiction especially, then

Can make of men the best or worst

With which earth can be blessed or cursed.

Poor work it is though, badly paid,—

Virtuous fictitious lies said

Fetch next to nothing, add to which,

Should writers make bad rhyming hitch,

Will sharply they be called to book,

To pieces instantly " be took "—

Be took! be took! oh, what grammar!

There! up goes the critical hammer,

You see, in a moment. " Be taken "

Like physic, I ought to be shaken)

Is but what I ought to have *said*,

This last word pronounce short, like *red* :

Not as before, where, mark the word *said*,

Long-drawn must be, to rhyme the word *paid*.

Thus oft have rhymsters to adapt

To circumstances words most apt

Their lines to rhyme. Thus with all things

Connected with human beings,

Circumstantial creatures are we,

From external influence free,

Seldom in our dealings through life,

In this keen aforesaid world's strife.

With respect to these two men now,

To their case return we somehow ;

When after the brandy they raced,

Temptation before them was placed ;

They said, " It sin was to waste it ; "

Asked, " Was it ordained they should taste it ? "

They drank, and as nothing it cost,

In drinking thought nothing they lost ;

But they did, by gaining instead,

(Like tiger, which once tastes blood red,)

Foul appetite, craving for more,

Oft creating a temptation sore,

To thieve—doubly with forbidden fruit,

When Possession desired follows suit

(Brandy was such) surely.

                    Instance Eve,

If that tale we are to believe,

Poor Adam's frail feminine half—

    At whom, ungallantly, some laugh,

Curse; saying " the sins of poor man,

But for her, would have never began,

Who than best, turned out the reverse,

Becoming poor Adam's worst curse ")—

Why Eve should have been first sinner,

Why Adam not the beginner,

None can quite see for to deceive

Is as easy quite, I believe,

Man as Woman —it all depends

On the temptation someone sends

Or offers.   Had very best gin
Before both been placed, to begin
Which first would have been, do you think,
To have taken the first hearty drink?
Perhaps Adam, to have saved Eve's fall,
Would have drank in self-sacrifice all,
For love of Eve, the whole bottle
Would have emptied down his own throttle.
Then, before that sinners we blame,
Let us well remember the same
Temptation that led them astray,
From virtue, that turned them wrong way.

But why should temptation be placed
Before man, to be thereby disgraced
By yielding thereto?   Man below,
The Almighty above must well know,
Beyond limit cannot resist
Temptation, unless God assist.
Then if man receives assistance,
What deserves man his resistance?
If unaided through weakness men fall,
Where lyeth the fault of it all?

It is all very fine to say
That man must not go the wrong way ;
If beyond man's strength man be tempt,
Then from blame must man be exempt.
Is not this clear logical fact,
To perceive which takes little tact ?
Yet some will put on a long face,
And say, I good morals disgrace,
When, simply, I wish but to shew,
Charity with judgment should go
Towards the fallen.
               For Example.
Where better could you find sample,
Than where said, " Go sin ye no more,
To the woman judgment brought for."

But tell me—How can sins limit be got ?—
As blend the colours of the rainbow,
Heaven and Hell as near together grow—
What one calls sin another does not !

All through own lens own deeds defend
In a Partial Prejudiced Way.
Where Saints begin and Sinners end,
— Elastic is Conscience—who can say ?

PART IV.

Animal! how much like are we!
At least of thoughts akin free
  And desires, each hath due share:
Thus Themeless a book have read you?—
The pivot on which novels, new
  And old, turn as much as they dare,
And Society Whirligigs
Hypocritical Extra Strong.

*　　　*　　　*　　　　　　*

Embryo Hero have we had.   To match
Want we for him a Heroine to catch.
Suppose there are none.   Then we must create
(Scribes can) a loving lass, who wants to mate.
Though Hero's one can easily define,
Yet not so easily a Heroine:
Heroine's should combine the virtues all;
Hero's need be, in tales, but handsome, tall;

What girl would love a short podgy Hero?
Love, at the very thought, sinks to zero.
Stands Love's Barometer, at short—fickle,
Nor can Hero's short—in tale—ladies tickle—
(Flattery is the Road Royal to success,
Truth ungarnished damns love-books, nothing less;
The soap-sentimental-soft-sawder-style,
Now-a-days suits best, is success' secret wile)—
Thus Hero's short—I defy contradiction—
Drawn Stumpy, would never do in fiction;
Therefore, Hero qualifications are but Two—
Handsome, Tall (regardless of what they do),
But Heroines—one and all Heaven bless them!—
Want carefully describing; well dress them;
Above all things (worldly) pretty let them be,
And (apparently) all simplicity—
Though were they this none would there be to fall,
Unseen dangers passed deserve no praise at all.
Without further preamble let me pen
The Picture of The Belle of Fairlight Glen.

Near to Fairlight Glen, once there stood
A white-washed cottage in a wood,

With roof mossed green.   Before the door
A trellised portico, all o'er
Covered with roses red, jasmine,
Honeysuckle sweet, eglantine,
And climbing plants of varied hue ;
Wildly intertwining, thus they grew
A Harmonious Contrast, Nature's Match,
Enlivening the ivy-green-clad thatch,
Amongst which sparrows chirruped and—fought—
Yes, quite true ; what they did not ought
To do, they did.   Thus oft do we ;
Ah ! when will from strife the world be free ?
Then, vieing with white gilder rose,
A moss-red rival in fullest blows,
(Or did) before glazed window.   A vine
Along the wall was trained in line,
From which, at autumn's fall, would hang
Ripe clusters, such as poets sang
Of (and will) since time immemorial.
The garden around pictorial,
With hyacinths, tulips, daisies pied,
Was stocked, each opening in due heed
To Dame Nature's Timely Season Call,
To bloom—to fade ; nor is that all,

But oft again in Nature's Course,
To bloom again with trebled force
Man Artificially Aiding.

Towards evening, when day was fading,
In portico, in old arm-chair,
Would sit its owner, shirt-sleeves bare,
The flower perfumes impregnating
With tobacco smoke, his ease taking.
Beside him would sit his loving wife,
Whom loved he dearer than his life;
Ay, with love stronger than that of youth,
Maturely ripened through years of truth
And companionship.   Her "old man,"
She called him—more loving term than
That he wanted not—it was enough—
Called polished terms "insincere stuff"—-
Never openly caressed her,
But ever mentally "God-blessed her."

One chick had they (Jane) a lovely lass,
For poor folk, *too lovely*—let that pass—
Who put under a case of glass

Should have been, she was so pretty.
(Excessive beauty, said pity,
Temptation is to be caressing
For fast young men too prone to pressing.)
To describe this Lass words would quite fail.
Then forgive if inkograph reads pale.

Her hair was golden, fine, yet strong,
Below her waist it reached thus long ;
Her eyes were blue as azure sky,
Admired by all the passers by ;
Cherry lips had she ; rose pink face ;
And tinge was seen of gipsy race
In her looks ; yet, she was as fair
As fairest could be found elsewhere ;
Small ; nor large ; yet had dainty waist
As round man's arm could there be placed :
In movement active, blithe, and gay ;
Possessed of pleasant, pleasing way
In manner, style, expression, walk ;
But, inclined somewhat to flirt in talk—
Forgive her this, she was so young,
It natural is to woman's tongue,
And why should it not be ?

For me,

Rather would I sit next a d——
Than dumby-girl, so goody-good,
Who could not flirt, but like-to would.

Flirtation is elegant strife,
   Of sexes agreeable battle,
Yet a harmless double-edged knife,
   Of meaningless tittle-tattle,
Sociable passage of wit,
Attempt at repartee, or hit,
With neighbour next whom you may sit.
Ride, walk, waltz, or converse a bit,
Exuberant youthful delight,
Enlivens a might-be dull night,
Dull care maketh quickly to fly,
Time merrily maketh slip by,
Dull youth better fitteth for life,
Ay, improves future husband and wife.
Young people indulge ye therein,
It never amounts to a sin,
As long as ye mean not deceive,
No heart will it ever make grieve —
Who words of flirtation believe?

When Helen was brought out quite young,
Around her youthful gallants hung.
She flirted with an active tongue,
   And she seemed most jolly.

Older, still is she maiden fair,
Nor gallant scorns as once she dare,
Though prettier grown, with pensive air
   A shade melancholy.

When Helen makes a change in life,
Will she not make the better wife,
Indulging in that youthful strife,
   Called flirtation folly ?

But we have not half Jane's charms quoted,
A few more must then here be noted.

Her teeth they were as white as pearl,
Her pretty lips possessed a curl
Like Cupid's Bow, somewhat haughty,
Though tempting, which some termed naughty—

(Dark Rivals, of course, such always were
Jealous of girls with golden hair ;
Who never otherwise have said,
Than " Golden hair *is* carrot red ; "
Whilst Golden angels retort back,
" You never yet saw hair jet black."
Thus varied beauties wage the war,
Thus will it be for evermore)—

But talk about small dainty feet
With insteps arched, it was a treat
To see hers. Then, a little higher,
Had ankles she that set on fire
All the masculines that saw them
Daintily trotting before them.
In fine, she was a pretty darling,
Unconsciously setting a-snarling
Open admirers, whilst, though sad,
She less favored fairies drove half mad.

To Lovers' Seat this Lass oft went
Alone, and there she often spent
Many an hour, where, High in Air,
She saw around, far, everywhere,

The fairest picture one could see
Of Nature's Subdued Majesty—
One of Nature's Modest Gems,
One of Natures Diadems,
That Crown this Earth to give delight
To gazers on the glorious sight.
High Rocks above, Deep Glen below
Where trees in softest verdure grow,
Varied in colour, size and shape,
To enhance in beauty Soft Landscape—
All interwoven, sweetly blended,
Through which Fond Lovers often wended
(A shade overrated, quite true,
By those who've seen no better view;
But there it is, as pretty spot
As in the county could be got).
Deep underneath is Open Sea,
Look straight beyond, there France should be;
Which, on a bright clear sunny day,
Is sometimes seen far, far away;
From whence the Robber Norman came,
And won of Saxon battle's game,
Fought near a thousand years ago,
Making rivers of blood to flow,

She wandered down the deep Glen oft,
Then up the Down reclimbed aloft.
Sometimes by Dripping Well would pass,
And drink therefrom a cooling glass
Of Nature's Nectar pure and white.
Sparkling like diamonds in sun light,
Reflecting rays, like liquid fire,
Yet cooler cup could none desire.

When summer sun, by shading trees,
(Through which oft played the zephyr breeze,)
Was softly subdued, there, at ease,

Under reclining she loved to lie,
Through opening gazing on blue sky,
Watching clouds weird-shaped, whirling by;

Seeing some cloud another chase,
As if upon dear life's death-race,
Until both vanish into space:

See others skid before the wind
Whilst sluggard lag and drag behind
Shapeless masses, like most cloud kind :

Whilst some would take familiar form,
Others foretell the coming storm,
Warning to shelter, dry and warm ;

See some with gold and silver lining,
Charity and Faith intertwining,
Hope Emblem for the sad repining,

Foretelling better days in store—
Spirit freed from foul carnal prison
Earth's Cares ended, Soul to Heaven risen—
God's Loving Gift—Life Evermore.

(Hope ! Hope ! Ah ! were it not for Hope,
Many an one would buy a rope,
Though what about strangulation,
Horrid thought, but worse sensation—
Och ! murther, pray such subject end,
Return we to our young fair friend.)

Loved Jane to listen to the song
Of lark on high, on wing so strong.

E

A sort of prayer it seemed to pray,
T'wixt heaven and earth it sang a lay
Of oft-repeated rhyme all day,
Twitt'ring, twitt'ring, twitt'ring away—

    I am a little lark,
    I carol in the sky,
        Oh! so high!
        Oh! so high!
    As Thanks for Mercies given,
    I sing aloft and raise
        Voice in praise,
        Voice in praise;
    Ask—"Ever grant us all,
    Self, little ones, and wife,
        Happy life,
        Happy life;
    Protect us from all harm.
    All danger drive away,
        Night and day,
        Night and day."
        Thus I sing,
        Thus I pray.

Yet oft my heart doth throb,
And tremble with dread fear,
　　When I hear,
　　When I hear,
Report of deadly gun,
Song with dread thought is stilled,
　　Who is killed?
　　Who is killed?
Oh! God, bleeding and dead,
There lies my little mate.—
　　Bairns all left,
　　Desolate!
Desolate! desolate!
Cruel sport! cruel fate!
　　Hush, hush, hush!
　　Sing no more,
　　Down I rush,
　　Killed! what for?
　　Killed! what for?

She loved to hear the cawing rook,
The linnet sing near "babbling brook,"
The wild ring doves gently cooing
In the woods, sweethearts a-wooing,

See swallows, swiftly skimming by,
Or congregate to homeward fly,
See butterfly erratic wing
Its course in sunshine ; and, in spring,
Hear cuckoo call from leafy tree,
Haunting the air most plaintively,
As if it knew it soon must say,
Cuckoo—cuck—stop short, then fly away ;
Hear plover call, " Pee wit," " Pee wit,"
Hear twittering wren, hear chattering tit,
Hear starling's wail, hear blackbird's note,
And bullfinch piping o'er the moat—
(Hear nightingale at eve, sombre, still,
And hooting owl, howl " whoop-poor-will ! ")—
Hear sing the yellow-hammer near,
The last notes drawling long, but clear,
The scale descending major third,
Weird minor talking songster bird ;—
" A little bit of bread, no, cheese-e-e-e,
I am so hungry, if you please-e-e-e—"
Contrasting with bold note of thrush,
That wonderful melodious rush
Of Nature's melody most sweet,
Of Nature a musical treat,

That Entrances the Soul, sets free
Thoughts on bird language mystery ,
As bird answers bird from distant tree,
Thus God *in* Nature hear and see,
God *and* Nature—Sweetest Poetry.

Yet in Nature even there are grades
Of sublime and laughable shades ;
Few see things with a Poet's eye,
Most look but at the food supply ;
Beef, mutton, pork, ducks, turkeys, "*geese*,"
Form poetry such minds best *please*,
Such call soul poetry " mind disease ; "
But some read poems in rough stones,
Whilst some minds grasp but picking bones,

Then like hounds, scent lost, hark we back
On trail proceed of prosy track.

Jane's father was a coastguardman,
Who oft the channel used to scan,
For smugglers, pirates, and odd fish,
Brown, rough, and somewhat outlandish.

He and his wife, folks both quite plain,
Their daughter christened simply Jane ;
Fine names were not then the fashion,
For which the world has now such passion.

Short retrospect now let us take,
Before of Jane a wife we make.
Four persons have already been
Brought in upon this love-tale scene ;
The teller of the tale late told,
The man three-score-and-ten years old ;
The coastguard man ; next, his plain wife ;
And Jane their dearest charm in life.

O'er him who fainted on the grass,
We quickly made his youth repass,
And left him where he just had learned,
That wealth by smuggling could be earned,
Quicker than by honest dealing,
Though some say " smuggling is not stealing
Exactly," yet cannot define,
Betwixt the two to draw the line.

This Lad and Lass together brought.

The others may be reckoned nought ;

Stop, the lads pa, I had forgotten

Long dead from drink, assume him rotten—

Oh! heavens! what vulgar words to use,

When trying hard to " do " the muse ;

What horrid thoughts they give rise to,

(Of that we here have nought to do).

But drop we now philosophizing,

And nauseous moralising ;

Leave that for professed guides to Above,

Love tales should only treat of love.

Then introduce to her first lover,

Jane Howard to Richard Glover ;

The same old man who fainting fell,

Whose life in youth we part did tell ;

Who fell in love with pretty Jane,

Who hers returned him for the same,

Who—

    Hold we must not pre-arrange,

All single girls have right to change,

Lest they contract by their marriage,

Of life's happiness—miscarriage—

Women have but one chance in life,
Best bargain making for a wife,
Except when loving husband dies,
They then can look for fresh supplies.

There! there! dear ladies be not cross,
Absent! thou art man's greatest loss,
I—I—do not mean half what I say,
In writing this I only play.

PART V.

Who is he?   Martial, lordly, ducal, stern,
Handsome, tall!—a mystery none could learn;
With stately step he grandly walked the street,
All eyes on him, such man, you seldom meet;
Moustached was he, and, with long flowing beard,
He looked quite fierce—angered much to be feared.
Some nobleman he must be people thought,
(For maiden grand prize by whom so e'er caught)
In the town at the head hotel he stayed,
Amongst the waiters grand commotion made,—
Waitaw—Yessaw—Dinnaw—Bring the wine list—
Yessaw; for such a man none dared resist;
Tall, handsome, martial, lordly, ducal, stern,
Who was he?   To know did not the yokels yearn;
Some said a Soldier Captain, or Sailor!—
But he only travelled for—a Tailor.

Was this Jane's sweetheart on love conquest bent ?
No, I merely draw a commercial gent,
Pitifully presumptious where e'er he went,
Probably bumptious on first journey sent—
Jane's sweetheart was Richard of whom I wrote.
First his old age and then his youth did quote,
How he saved then loved Jane soon will I note.

As if retiring for night's rest,
The sun was sinking in the west,
Shedding straight streams of golden light
In sort of pleasant dreams good night
Parting, but others to surprise
With silver beams in mornings' rise.

Thus has the sun two sets of rays
Morn's call to work—eve's call to praise,
As one begins the other ends,
Yet into each, each softly blends
Smoothly gradual, yea so true,
Ah, wonderful ! yet who that knew,
Nature to ever make mistake,
(Though freaks most strange it oft doth make)

During the millions and millions
Ay, billions heaped upon billions
Of years that have the sun and world
Into eternal space been hurled.
As they began—stopping never—
Thus will they go on ever, ever.
Ah! First, First Beginning who can
Say when that beginning began.

Ay! First, First Beginning who can
Say when that beginning began;
From nothing the world came say some—
From nothing but nothing can come;
The world is made up of matter—
But from nothing can come this latter;
Matter grows, increases, some state,
Universally No, nor Abate
Can matter so—it but shifts place,
As it changes about in space;
Than Adam was man long before
As matter, but which by God's Law
But changed form from what it had been
And as man was thereafter seen—

Result of chemical changes,

That by which God prearranges ;

God is Nature, Nature—Chemistry,

Yet neither solves the Mystery

Of First Beginning, for from a sod,

If God made man, then who made God ?

Self cannot self make for we know,

Self first must exist to do so ;

Yet a first must have been in things all,

To existence that first first to call ;

No man man's beginning can say,

Perhaps might could he spirit waylay,

Chemically analyze soul,—

Life-germ of the animate whole ;

Yet of that man need not despair,

Science secrets daily lays bare,

Grand results doth daily disclose,

Shewing man wiser much daily grows,

And that somewhat, probably later,

May he learn from his great Creator.

Life germ mystery—but then, then,

Who made God will remain as when

Man problem first started—unanswered.

Yet God gave man logic that he
Man's creation might one day perhaps see,
Found out it would only but raise
For His wondrous works but more praise.
Yet at science raileth the blind
Such things say we ought not out find,
Thus ignorance calls science fool,
Because it would find out God's rule
Secret, and, by keen reason's gift,
Beginning of man's being sift.

God purposely planted desire
In man's breast that he might enquire
Of His hidden wonders untold,
His secret mysteries unfold,
And now man has developed in mind,
As from infant grown to mankind,
Of Chemistry now somewhat grasps,
(Part Godhead) and still for more gasps.
Mind-Instinct it is now that man
Should enquire, but how he began.
Yet however much wiser he grows,
He must own still little he knows ;

For, should he his origin learn—then
Who made God will remain as when
He problem first started—unsolved,
For, for therein there is involved
The logic of God Himself solely,
Beyond man, perplexing wholly.
Ah! First, First Beginning, who can
Say when that beginning began ?
Eternity of human soul
Compared to First Infinite Whole
Of God, the Universe, is youth green—
Green ! except to such as may have been
Created coeval.

    Too far-fetched,
However, has mind to be stretched
To grasp such subject, and when got,
By most is appreciated—not.
The doings of humanity,
In its blind, blind insanity,
Are enough, with its vanity,
Mankind mostly to interest—
Mankind prefers vanity best,
And thoughts of lesser moment.

Then back again hie we to earth
To suit those minds of lesser birth.

As sun was sinking in the west,
Passed Richard Glover, sailor-dressed,
Along the shore, near Lovers' Seat,
That most romantic Love's Retreat—

Here, intrude I must, this love-tale sweet,
Quite foreign to Richard and Jane,
To whom soon return we again,
But first—
The Tale of Lovers' Seat:— *
Immortalizing Miss Boys' feat,

---

* For the particulars of the above story, connected with Lovers'
Seat, relating to Miss Boys and Captain Lamb, I am indebted to a
little girl whom I found solitarily occupying one of the seats belong-
ing to this far-famed romantic retreat, so rural and rustic, and who
appeared to be about ten or twelve years of age.

She wore a coarse straw hat, very much the worse for wear, with
a wide brim, and had on a pinafore that was, to say the least, not as
white as it ought to have been, considering how recently it appeared
to have been washed and mangled. Her *tout ensemble* was the
counterpart of that class of beggars who get themselves up expressly
to excite pity by trying to mislead the charitable with the idea that

From whence, when married, at death of Lamb

Her husband, cast she herself to jam—

He having near the Isle of Wight,

In liquor, drowned himself one night—

Midst rocks below.   A Captain bold

Was Lamb when living, I am told,

For loss of whom his wife did court

Death for a wedded life too short.

---

if they are poor, nevertheless they are clean, and therefore, perforce, industriously inclined, but, unfortunately, are suffering from the effects of having "no work to do;" whereas, if any were offered to them, they would in all probability refuse it, knowing full well that begging not only suits their lazy and vagrant dispositions better, but pays best. This poor girl was evidently what is termed "got up" for the *role* she had to play.   Pity her we may, for doubtless her parents were to blame for all her failings; but to pity them would, I think, be a stretch of just benevolence whomsoever they may have been.

With a view to relieve the restraint I fancied my advent had put upon the child, I made some casual remark.   She made no reply, but only gave me in return a repulsive, semi-vacant, uncouth stare, which only impressed me with an idea that she possessed indifferent parentage.   Instinctively I had felt this before I spoke to her, by her general appearance and manners, for children but reflect the examples set them, and that unconsciously.   Further observation only tended to confirm me in my judgment: and, after mentally expressing pity for her and her imagined unfortunate nativity, I took no further interest in the child for the time.

Poor young widow! Pity extend—

Self-sacrifice (?)—Love's fitting end.

But alas! for her, she rescued was,

By another gentleman, because

He happened to be passing by,

Who, at the moment, cocked his eye,

Presently a middle-aged gentleman arrived on the scene.

Shortly after, two ladies, escorted by another gentleman, followed, and after having taken a good survey of the scenery around, above, and beneath them, all sat themselves quietly down.

Watching a favourable opportunity, the child sprang up, and taking off her hat, stood in front of the company present: but, heedless of her danger, so near to the edge of the precipice, as to make my blood curdle lest she should take another step backwards to be smashed to atoms below. She then repeated in a monotonous sing-song recitative tone, a rigmarole, the substance of which I reduce to rhyme. But I am bound to add the two lines—

> The shells of the ocean shall be my bed,
> That shrimps may wiggle-waggle o'er my head,

are, as near as I can possibly remember, literally hers. Yet I will not swear she may not have said "lobsters" in her distinct indistinctness of recital. I have, however, well considered the refreshing but troublesome (unless previously skinned) substantive since, and am still inclined to think shrimps was the word, they being much more likely to "wiggle-waggle" than lobsters, except in company with bottled stout and excursionists when on the cruise.

Immediately she had finished she came round with her hat, but in a manner which plainly said—

"If you don't give me something, be hanged to you."

F

And saw this lady hanging there,

Clinging to bough of tree mid-air.

Could she have chosen fitter time

In which to do this deed sublime?

————————————— ————

This occurred about the middle of the day. The gentleman who first arrived on the scene gave her a shilling, for which she gruffly grunted, "Thank'ee," but without attaching the shadow of a "sir" thereto. She then presented, or rather shoved her hat towards me. I had no coppers, and not feeling inclined, from the impression that she had created, to be over liberal, but yet not wishing to let my prejudice overcome my benevolence—perhaps unjustly—I compromised with my conscience thus, by handing her sixpence, and requesting her to return me threepence out. With a bad grace she made a dive into her pocket, when, lo and behold! she hauled therefrom a handful of silver and copper that must have amounted in the aggregate to at least ten or fifteen shillings. Feeling surprised that a child so young should be trusted at so solitary a spot with so much money, I asked her "how she came by it?"

She but gave a cunning, leering grin in reply. Feeling curious, I told her if she would tell me she might keep the sixpence.

Considering for a moment, as if fearing she might be compromising herself, she said—

"Genelmen and ladies gives it me wot comes here. That's wot they guv me this morning."

I then told her she might keep the sixpence, but received not a grunt of thanks therefor. Feeling pitifully annoyed at her ill-manners and ingratitude, I, by way of chaff, asked her her name. Not forthcoming, I told her I would give her another sixpence if she

He did not stay himself to ask,

Or question self-inflicted task ;

To the rescue he quick rushed,

Through the underwood crashed crushed ;

---

could spell it, hoping for the child's sake she might be able to do so
She immediately began—

"F-E—FE—B-PHŒBE Y-T—WHITE. PHŒBE WHITE."

"Bravo!" I mentally exclaimed, "evidently a disciple of the new
Spelling Reform." I then asked her her father's name.

"Philip," she said.

I asked her to spell it, which she did thus—

"F-I-L-L-U-P."

"Bravo!" I mentally exclaimed again, being now fully confirmed
in my suspicions as to which or what college she was indebted.

She now went with her hat to solicit of the two ladies. They gave
her nothing, but their escort (evidently, like myself, not prepossessed
in her favour) gave her, or rather threw her, a penny.

Transferring the penny from her hat to her eye, she fixed it therein
(the gentleman sported a single eye-glass), gave a derisive laugh, then
looking the trio in the face, with a leer from the other disengaged
eye, said sneeringly, referring to the gift of but a penny for the party—

"A farden apiece and one over—yah!"

The surprise of the donor must be imagined.

*　　*　　*　　*　　*　　*

What I now add has, however, no connection with the above-
mentioned incident: but having had my fill of the glorious beauties of Lover's Seat, I continued my walk through a lovely grove
towards Fairlight Down, until I came to a pasture surrounded almost
entirely by woods, in about the middle of which stood a wooden

And though she took some time to reach—
Happily for both she stuck like " leech "—
He saved her. Then, of course, they married ;
But little time having tarried,

---

built hut, devoted to the sales of refreshments of a light nature, and
upon the door of which hung a board placarding the announcement,
"New Milk." Instantly I thirsted. New milk, who would not
thirst for new milk in such an 'innocent looking spot, I wondered,
where country cows were actually grazing in full sight, ay, and
within a stone's throw. Cows upon whose features were stamped
virtue and innocence so plainly, that I verily believed had a London
milkman entered the pasture they would have butted him with indig-
nation. Yes, instantly I thirsted, added to which the day was hot and
I had sojourned long. There was plenty of London labelled lemonade
looking one full in the face; but who—from London especially—
would not scorn that fictitious fizzle. I did at least, and as no one
else was there, the rest of the company did also. I ordered milk,
which was handed to me by a damsel whose ruddy cheeks incon-
testably announced her to any but the least imaginative, a natural
born milkmaid pure and simple. Mentally, I saw her sitting on a
low stool with her head firmly butted into the cow's side, whilst I
heard the milk going into the pail with a whiz-phiz-whiz-phiz, as
regularly as clockwork, as she vigorously alternatively and perse-
veringly tugged and squeezed away. No sooner did I receive the
milk (a good half-pint glass well filled) than down it went at a
draught before as much as I had once tasted its flavour. Ordering
another, I then sipped and drank it leisurely. Ah, it was milk !
Having finished that I then made a heavy onslaught upon a miscel-
laneous selection of puffs, tarts, sponge cakes (the devil seize that

Before they tied the loving knot,

In remembrance of the dangerous spot,

Though she had said, when poor Lamb died,

" She never would again get tied

piano next door, if it is not veritable his majesty, or his wife, or his daughter, or the two latter, already in possession—who can write with that fiendish noise—that supernatural screeching—dinging through one's ears—

Oh, sweet spirits hear my prayer,
Shut your windows down with care.
To hear piano and voice fight
Is not welcome day and night,
For never hear I both agree,
The melody or harmony
Except in ff's, aye, double three.)—

and other delicacies, and which I liberally divided with the wasps, of which there appeared to be a nest or nests somewhere near. I however, felt very grateful they did not sting me, although I could not help secretly feeling they very much wanted to do so, by their assiduous attentions. Sponge-cakes and jam puffs swallowed whole-sale hastily having a propensity to rise, I thought the best thing I could do would be to put another glass of milk upon the top of them to keep them down; and so I did. I then sat myself down to enjoy a cigar, previously ordering another glass of milk. Having leisurely finished both, I then felt comfortable, and commenced my walk anew, feeling also an inward conviction that I had done my duty in patronizing my quadrupedial feminine fellow-creatures, the aforesaid kine, so picturesquely and peacefully grazing around me. Thoughts followed on the beauties of the simplicity and innocence attached to a rural life, and I was just

To another," though once having vowed

(Ere she tried suicide) aloud—

The shells of the ocean shall be my bed,

That shrimps may wiggle waggle o'er my head.

Childless she was I forgot to say,

With Captain Lamb, but not that way

---

getting into a romantic vein, when, scarcely a hundred yards from the wooden hotel I had just left, what should stare me full in the face but a veritable pump. Could it be a mental vision, or was I lacteally intoxicated ? No ; it was a pump. Then I hoped there might be no well attached; but my hopes sank to zero, when I thought how absurd it would be to place a pump otherwise than in connection with a well. Still I felt I must convince myself, and I therefore approached the machine with a view to test its efficacy. With a timid heart I lifted the handle, then plucking up courage, which grew plentifully around me, I suddenly pushed the handle down, when, simultaneously, out rushed a stream of water from its spout that would have induced any London milkman—so rich was it—to have purchased it there and then on the spot, to have been transferred to London thereafter, with the hope of making an immense fortune thereby. My heart sank a foot or two. With terrible misgivings (until I felt dreadful cramping creeping pains somewhere between the regions of my head and the soles of my feet), but one association of ideas engrossed me for the rest of the day, viz.,—pumps and cows—cows and pumps—water and milk— milk and water—the country in London—London in the country— London milk in the country—London dodges in the country, with finally—oh ! humiliating thought—Londoners thereby sold--done brown, aye milk and watered. I had a dreadful ache all that day and the next, but not in the head.

When she wedded a second time,
And heard St. Clement Dane's sweet chime
Again.   Happy they were after,
Of course, number one's disaster
I need not say.   Thus ends the Story
Tragical, of Lover Seat Glory.

Again to our tail—tale I mean,
But never mind, the School Boards seem
To think, it matters not so much,—
That Phonetics the other from such
Must determine.   (I wonder how
Will end the present spelling row!)

As sun was sinking in the west—
Bother the sun; give us the rest
Quickly; tiring is this same line
Oft repeated; why not define
Your story without digressing?
To patience it is distressing!

Dear Reader, I apologize.
But pray let not your choler rise,

Did I not say this tale would run
Ramblingly ere I scarce begun?
Rambletonia! what means it?
And Hastingsonia, to wit?
Both figure on the title-page,
Then calmly get not in a rage;
If first the end you wish to learn,
The last page read, and backward turn.
But surely you are not a skipper,
Possessing the soul of a slipper;
I mean, excuse me, nothing rude,
And hope I shall not be construed
As such; I only try to pile
The agony up for awhile,
As writers generally do,
By reserving the grand tableau
For the last, as in pantomime,
Or tales written for Christmas time.

But disappointed should you be
With tale and rhyme, judge leniently:
Pretend I not to be Shakespear,
Nor to approach at all him near;

But if a Shakespear I am not,
Some consolation can be got
In the knowledge that none there are
His like (sad thought) by very far.
Oh, Shakespear! of Poets king of kings,
Immortalized of human beings,
Forgive me naming thy great name
In words, to thine, so awful tame,
Though I tug hair for rhyming shoots
Of Greek, Latin, Anglo-Saxon roots

(Laugh at the joke, it is an age
Of quips, plays, extravaganzas sage,
And witty weak weeklies of wit,
With caricatures pencilled to fit); *

* CAPITAL " PUZZLES.

P ersonalties petty on folks,
U nspeakable coarse cuts, witless jokes.
N ever once the mark hitting in ten,
C ommonplace, at its best, even then—
H yperbolical pencil and pen.

N ot downwards—upwards read these three letters,
U ndoubtedly much worse than its betters
P or true wit, to which few are deep debtors.

But, no more let me my tale disjoint,
If I can, come I now to the point.

As sun was sinking in the west,
Passed Richard Glover, sailor-dressed,
Up Fairlight Glen, near Lovers' Seat,
To Dripping-Well fast flying fleet.
He scream had heard from woman's throat—
Jane's—a not to be mistaken note,
" Ex-cel-si-awr ! " he fiercely cried,
Then towards the spot he quickly hied,
Like Miss B.'s husband number two—

Stop !   What on earth am I writing,
Excelsior ! to be inditing ?
Forgive me, I—am—so—tired, to bed
I now must send my muddled head.
To-morrow, without fail, shall you hear,
How Richard saved his sweetheart dear.
Now, take I what I did not " oughter,"
A nightcap still of gin and water,
And then may follow (who knows ?) dreams
Upon this said young lady's screams,

Illustrating tales (hem !) untold,
Of how *our pa's*, when young and bold,
Tickled *our ma's* under the chin,
Which, now-a-days, ma's would think sin
For younger persons to commit—
Young persons now-a-days doth sit,
Demurely cultivating mind,
Eschewing sex of other kind,
Leaving frivolity behind,
Best goody goody's— of their kind."

PART VI.

Papa had been a banker rich, rolling in heaps of gold,
But by some rogue conspirators had been completely sold;
Broken hearted, he lived not long, pity the poor old man;
Mamma, quite broken hearted too, to follow soon began;
Sweet Isabel alone was left, to live in anguish keen,
Then, up till then, at grandest ball, she reigned acknow-
       ledged queen;
Now, bold admiring titled courtiers, disappeared aye all,
No loss such loss, true, say you, but, it softens not downfall;
For, except to those, who once have been, as rich as rich
       can be,
None know the pangs of rich downfall to genteel poverty,
Though from the wreck there may be left what some would
       call wealth quite,
Yet lessened circumstances make life's battle hard to fight.

The taunt, the sneer, cold shoulder given from bosom
friends of late,
Incline the heart from love, if left, to pardonable hate ;
Half imperceptibly we climb the ladder of this life,
But when we fall therefrom we find, begins worse up hill
strife—
Heart-rending, terrible, discouraging, spirit crushing,
Which oft, aye sad, sad, too oft, setteth soul hellward
rushing ;
Charity inciting, help inviting,—Oh ! to such expand
Ye who are able, if for heaven you wish, a helping hand.

❖ ❖ ❖ ❖ ❖

Oh !   Could I write words something new,
But Solomon said, truly true,
" There's nothing new under the Sun : "
Yet this phrase is, if not neater,
" The world is but a round repeater,"
More—" All things are now overdone."

Thus Nature pulsates, throbs, and beats,
In circles it itself repeats ;
Next, Nations do the same likewise,
They rise to fall, but fall to rise

Individuals do much the same,

An Instance see, though very tame :—

Authors (oh my !) repeat themselves,

Ay ! some but take from musty shelves

Old books of tales which they regild,

And, publish them as their own build ;

Or does the idyosyncratic

Useless publisher dogmatic ;

Useless except to collar gains,

Publishers live on authors' brains ;

At least, some do, that I know well,

I would, but that I dare not, tell ;

Ah ! never will I in future go

To —— and —— or —— and Co.,

Above all, ye gods quill pen, beware !

Of a certain Piccadilly Bear.

Thereby hangs tale, I must relate

(Oh ! thieves I do abominate,)

Discourteous ones most of all,

Publishers—tallest of the tall.

An author once to one applied

("Tis truth and cannot be denied),

Publisher saw, who to him said,

" By us your work must first be read,"

In tones so sweet the author thought,
His work he had to angel brought,—
(Oft having experienced before
How P's treat Authors by the score),
But the work no sooner had he got
Than shewed he his teeth, a biting lot;
Confidingly, the author left
MSS., not dreaming a theft,
Of it's contents would copied be.
Circulated in journals free.
The book's contents, when made quite stale,
Then wrote the Publisher " *your tale*
 Will pulish we for——" (such a sum
Would leave author nought, P. the plum)—
" *As we fail to see therein aught new* "
And which, of course was very true
For, Contents pirated and sold
Had in a journal been pre-told.

But that nought is new under the Sun !
Yea, truly things are over done !
Though this old saw is seldom heard,
(Saws, dogmas, never are absurd),

Mouthed by wits at every chance,
"They better do these things in France,"
Do they?   Suppose we thereat glance.

In France, I hear, no female heart
Ever for loss of male doth smart ;
There ladies sell it by the pound
To highest bidder to be found ;
Yes! they better do these things in France,
As plainly seen at such a glance ;
Nor do " femmes " there an action lance,
For breaches, I am told.

Now mark ye the difference between
French heart, and English heart, so green ;

In England ladies sell not that,
If little hearts go pit-a-pat
At sight of every wealthy man,
Pity their owners, if you can,
For, in self-disinterestedness
Wed English women and rich men bless.

But is that aught new under the sun ?
Oh, dear no—yea, things are overdone,

Except—except, Love, except Love,
Heart sedative from, say, above.
Love, cannot be o'erdone in tales,
To please the girls Love never fails ;
Pile up the sweet stuff hot and strong,
Girls love Love Tale, nor care how long.

But even Love itself repeateth,
So with lovers who oft meeteth,
There is little deviation
In Love Tales, the same cleave-i-a-tion
In the end, 'tis but the old, old, groove
Repainted wherein lovers move —
The same old, old. story—The pain
Of broken hearts made whole again.
Than such agony what more severe,
To lose a heart that once cost dear,
Save the pieces, the heart must break,
Unless, some other heart it take ;
To broken heart, is broken head
Trivial—so easily mended—
Run to the nearest doctor's shop,
And plaster up the wounded top ;

But not so with a broken heart.

'Tis hard to realise the smart.

Heart is so tender and so soft.

Oh cruel ! it is to break it oft,

O'er its fracture lament, deep, deep.

There is but one cement, (weep ! weep !)

Homœopathic in its action,

Which can mend the broken fraction :

Successfully such case to meet,

Here followeth the best receipt—

Ry.

    Sim. Similibus Curanter—

Apply another heart, instanter,

Pierce them both through with Cupid's skewer,

And then to make a perfect cure,

Both let the parson quickly wed

Two into one in heart and head ;

Then never after will they part,

Unaided by the lawyers art.

I fancy I hear young ladies say,

" Shame! shame ! to write of heart that way.

And, so it is my pretty dears,

Forgive, I am but young in years,

Offend I, regret I, I spoke,
Please bear in mind I do but joke ;
This book is written but in fun,
With now and then, thought serious one.

Where we left off then, now return—
Jane's scream—nor soft, and there we learn,
Poor girl! she dropped down Dripping Well ;
Now, why she did it, let me tell ;
But first, particular notice take,
She did it for none other's sake
Save her own, that against her will,
Happily receiving little ill,
Although end might have been severe,
Had not, luckily, help been near.

Old Dripping Well, please bear in mind,
To present was of different kind ;
Of water-fall there now is little,
Barely enough to downward trickle,
Except, perhaps, in wet winter time,
Then much more muddy than sublime.
But, in olden time, a mighty stream,
Was crossed by rough uneven beam,

Which stream rushed down a giddy height,
And by its weight, which gave it might,
Formed seething treacherous pool below,
Sure death for those who in should go.
Down ! down ! the water used to pour !
In loudest thunder's deafening roar !
Causing the spray in steam to rise !
In clouds that reached up to the skies !

At least, this is what they told me ;
Inclined am I to think they sold me,
I say, lest, when you see the spot,
You say, I have drawn it rather hot.

Quite, is Dripping Well, from the shore,
A quarter of a mile or more ;
Wind, gentle drifting scream aright,
Fully explains the happy sight,
Of youthful manhood on rescue bent,
Yelling Excelsior ! as he went.

As Jane was stepping rustic bridge,
Her foot slipped off its narrow ridge ;

She gave one scream, began another,
Which culminated in a smother;
She sank deep once, soon up she came,
Went down again, twice up the same,
And now to rescue Glover came,
And Richard was his Christian name.

Thus do I particularize
That none may say, with feigned surprise,
Your tale, it does not tally quite,
With what you said the other night
When you indulged in—you know what—
What? Gin and water, strong and hot.

Perhaps some may say, "How funny it seems
He should have gone with so few screams
Direct to this—this very Well"—
Well—so it does; but—who can tell
Whether fate did his footsteps guide
To where Jane almost suicide
Committed accidentally,
By falling off that fallen tree?—
(Aforesaid rustic bridge placed thwart
The stream by strong wind one day caught).

Just one word more before we end
All discrepancies to defend ;
Writers, at trifles must not stop,
Or would they have to shut up shop,
Through difficulties they may slip
With a jump, hop, or long, long skip ;
Hair breadth escapes that will not wash !
May be styled dreams ! hush ! Say not "bosh,"
Though easier is it to condemn
Best tale than write the worst of them.

But soon, no doubt, all tales will be
Imagined by Machinery
By the million—oh ! horrid thought !
For authors poor, without an ought.

PART VII.

WHAT Guides
North, South, West, East,
With other hemispheres
In universal endless space
Wherein is quite incomparably small
This earth ?   Are other worlds, each one and all,
Alike peopled with kindred race
Possessed of Hellish fears,
Heaven hopes, High Priest,
Besides ?

Strong, strong,
Questions of doubt ;
Then according to curse,
Or God's Love, as some preachers preach,
Which way through Space Infinite, without end,

Or beginning, shall soul from this earth wend,
Heaven High or Hell Deep to reach,
For better or for worse ?
Death ! may find out
Ere long.

Heaven High
(Or Hell Deep) reached,
What will man's Soul do there?
Nauseous sickening praises sing
For evermore?   Can God have created man
And vast worlds for no other purpose than
To praise or ever be cursing ?
The Logic of Despair,
By mad Mind preached
Surely !

Mind ! Mind !
Given the Rein,
Where wouldst thou wander to?
Yea ! to beyond regions forbidden.
Forbidden ! By whom ? What ? Man's Cowardice !
Mind fears to tread, like Man, on untried ice,

Lest it open to horrors hidden.
Yet Mind will deep thoughts woo,
Ever attain,
Out find.

*　　　　*　　　*　　　*

I once heard that a man jumped deep
Into water, and in death's sleep
Was well advanced ; that, when brought round,
To life restored, he then fault found
With those who saved him.   Left alone,
He said, he would never have known
He had passed through death's sensation ;
Which, to the imagination,
Is frightful, supposed to last long,
The mind with dread thoughts to o'erthrong.
He further said, that soul's relief
From body was beyond belief ;
By which he believed heaven to be,
Spirit released of body free ;
And from what of Future he had seen,
Said, " Life is here on earth, I ween,

Hell or Purgatory—Man Doomed
To walk this earth with Soul entombed
In bodily tormentation
Of flesh,—that the termination
Of the Soul's fleshly interment
Was the end of man's punishment ;
Of happy future to be spent
The beginning."

        Thus wicked, he said,
Nor thanks gave for rescue from the dead.
Yet this talk so his friends impressed,
Each then commenced to get undressed
To jump in also, end to make ;
But, when this man began to take
Homeward direction, they home went,
Saving their lives by courage spent,
For, " Why not jump in again," growled they,
" If in such bliss he wished to stay ? "

Was Jane ungrateful, like this man,
To him who to her rescue ran ?
After her bath, ere she came round,
He stretched her on a grassy mound ;

And, as soon as he her beauty saw,

(Which was perfection without flaw)

Instantly became her lover,

Did this brave youth, this Richard Glover.

He then unhooked her gown behind,

(Now fashions are of different kind)

Her neck and bosom both laid bare,

Exposing to the freshening air,

(The quicker that she might come round)

Then, listening for expectant sound

Of breath, and life return again,

Whilst chafing, sat admiring Jane,

Unconsciously she moved, but, shocking!

She exposed her legs and stocking;

This sight was more than he could bear,

For legs with features would compare,

It cooked his goose, it settled him,

But non-possession nettled him.

He cautiously then peered around,

Then kneeled he down upon the ground

And stole a kiss, another took,

Then at more charms had secret look,

She moved her lips as if to speak,

He kissed again her soft pale cheek;

Her bosom then began to move,

As if these deeds she did approve.

Transfixed, enraptured at the sight,

He fell in love with all his might ;

Half hoped she would not yet awake

That he of charms might still stock take.

About to take another kiss

Of this fair beauty, pretty miss,

He at the thought of that dread word,

Pale turned quite, then thought, pshaw, absurd !

That one so young should married be,"

Hoped yet to wed she might be free,

Then, quickly glancing at left hand,

" Thank heaven," he sighed, " no wedding band

Is there," then vowed, " she shall be mine,

Let all the world against combine,"

Truly " according to Cocker,"

Thoughtless of a shot in the locker.

Heaving and falling and trying,

Life to win back, gently sighing,

Her bosom more and more expanded,

As life returned, where once half-stranded ;

And she began to move somewhat

Before full-consciousness she got.

First, she half-opened both her eyes,

Next, them fully opened in surprise,

A moment looked about in wonder,

But when she heard the water thunder

As it poured and roared down Dripping Well,

She then remembered how she fell.

She did not ask, she did not dare,

" Oh! where am I?"   Her bosom bare

Itself presenting, shocked her sight,

Blushed she with modest maiden might,

To think a stranger should be there,

To see her dormant founts quite bare ;

Gave sudden jump, and then essayed

To gain her feet, but backwards swayed,

And in strong arms there fainting fell,

Though far from strong, yet close to Well.

He took her in his brawny arms,

Displeased not at her weighty charms,

Carried her to the nearest cot,

Found her's it was when there they got,

Where lived her Pa, the coastguard man,

A Telescopic Guardian.

Pa was out, on smuggling duty,

When this young brave brought home the beauty,—

Keeping watch for brandy smugglers,

And other such dishonest jugglers—

Ma was not, gave she a woman's shriek,

(Which oft resembles grunters squeak)

A rush made at her darling child,

(Like quarrelsome men when over wild)

Asked lots of questions all in one

Before reply could be begun

Of explanation, or behaviour,

Of Jane and her devoted saviour.

He placed Jane in " that old arm chair "—

Sofas in those days were rare,

The lowly then fast kept their place,

With richer seldom tried to race,

As now through unions (Trade) since began

Ruination of the working man.

Now would-be gents we but have left,

Of working men we are bereft

Except their masters are behind them.

Where now workmen will you find them ?

Workmen British, ha ! ha ! forsooth

Heaven help me, but I must speak truth,

Except it is the same to shirk
(Fool flattered pigs) they will not work !
Of sympathy deserving none
As a body their wages won (?)
In drunkenness spending, that done,
Achieved, with behaviour of beast,
Bank holidays, Fast days, and Feast.
Street-swearing non-provident lot,
Too often habitual sot
Than sober exception to rule,
Starving wife beaters oh ! cruel,
Ugh ! horrid ! the oaths in every street,
Loud disgusting, from some we meet ;
Foul language, to which oaths are mild,
Assail the ears of every child :
Pity enforced is not the law,
To punish dirty foul-mouthed jaw.

There, now, how do you like these truths,
Ye working men, ye manly (?) youths ?
Let me be not misunderstood,
I simply fault find for your good ;
If I your finer feelings sting,
It self-improvement perhaps may bring :

I hope I may not wound in vain,
At least. from dirty speech refrain,
Know—speech refined is golden gain.

Now, let me give you sound advice,
Though my remarks may not be nice;
Choose. ye working men, best leaders,
Discard ye all dishonest pleaders
Such, of late, as did not report
Dishonest frauds as leaders ought.
Real Friends flatter not—take heed,
Leaders should be in word and deed
Just in all to men and masters—
Whom thank ye men, for your disasters?
By bad advice for greedy pay,
Sure, have you been misled, I say,
Your strikes have stricken trade away,
Our English Trade has had its day,
But Agitators! what care they?
Men, they laugh at you; well they may,
Quarry have You been!—They Birds of Prey!
To benefit both man and nation,
Teach we the working man his station,

Nor crush, favor, unduly raise,
Beyond his worth by clap-trap praise).

But to our Tale return we where,
He placed Jane in the old arm-chair,
And left her to her mother's care,
Saying, with looks bereft of sorrow,
"I'll call and see yer gal to-morrow,"

Before, however, this he said,
Jane had been warmly put to bed ;
And, before she went that night upstairs,
Her Ma perceived how stood affairs ;—
That Richard to Jane had lost his heart,
That Jane of hers re-gave a part.
How this she learned is quickly told,
Lovers look fools, both young and old,
In looks too hot or else too cold,
Too sweetly mild to last, nor bold,
Lest each one might perchance be sold
When dove-tailed by that ring of gold.

Thus parents quickly find love out
When lovers love without a doubt ;
But youngster lovers never mind,
Your Ma's and Pa's once did same kind,
Nor secret keep, nor be afraid,
To own your love if heart has strayed !
All secret courtship doubtful ends,
Oft makes worst foes of once best friends.

It was intended from Above
That man and woman each should love ;
Love is a thing none can control,
Self generates from inmost soul,
Fiercer it burns, towards kindred flies
As passion with time as surely dies ;
Though spurned, to deadly hate it turns,
Yet true love ever slightly burns ;
Love never dies, the spark once lighted,
But smoulders still, however blighted,
Easily fanned into fresh flame
By owner of the first loved name.

Yet time works wonders, none can tell
When after death comes wedding bell.

Ah! what ups and downs make up this life,

To-day a widow, to-morrow wife,

For widows, as wise Weller said,

Soon knock their courting on the head

Once widows woo, they quickly wed.

But then, why should they not do so?

It was not meant to be all woe,

And pull long faces here below,

When to another world friends go!

However much in life loved dear,

Yet for lost love the constant tear

Would never do in this world here;

Friends would call you chicken-hearted

To ever mourn the dear departed;

And friends are so sympathizing,

Kind-hearted and moralizing,

And reticent in advertising

One's faults, others them advising.

No! No! it would not do all weeping,

And for ever griefs be keeping

Green, evergreen, in the bud,

When friends are buried in the mud!

Then forward look, forget all pasts,

Be merry here whilst life it lasts—

Yet think of the morrow not, some say !
Hem—Well—avoid extremes either way ;
The Happy medium always take,
The wisest course for each one's sake.

PART VIII.

—o〜o—

Young.

Alone sit I thinking,
A Cup of Tea Drinking,
With Curtains Drawn Tightly,
Whilst fire blazes brightly,—
What will my future be?

Old.

Alone sit I thinking,
A Cup of Tea Drinking,—
My youth hath passed o'er me
With short life before me ;
Ah ! could we the future see !

Dead.

Sombre mourners sit thinking,
Whilst eating and drinking,—

Oh! did I offend her?
Too carefully tend her?
What has she left to me?

*　　　*　　　*　　　*　　　*

The Old Coastguard came home to tea,
Regularly always did he,
Then filled his pipe, began to smoke,
Before his wife to him once spoke,
Of Jane's adventure and downfall,
And rescue by the young man, tall.

The old man listened to the tale,
At first with brown face turned quite pale;
But when he heard how Jane was saved,
For young man's name he almost raved,
That he might him his best thanks tend,
Towards whom he felt indebted friend.
Few know the feelings of a father!
(Mothers may a little, rather)
For lost child saved! restored again!
From deep accumulated rain.
The man was overjoyed with pleasure,
He loved the man who saved his treasure,

His darling child, to him life's charm,
Who thus was plucked from water's harm.

" Who is this man ?   What is his name? "
He breathless said ; " I do you blame,
You did not ask him wait for me,
That I might heartfelt thanks give free
To him, who saved Jane, our daughter,
From Dripping Well's dangerous water."

"Ma" then to " Pa " full all related,
And what she guessed she also stated :
For long before Pa had returned
Ma mentally wedded both, now yearned
To hear the wedding bells set pealing,
To soothe her agitated feeling.
For with ladies all the wedding ring
Absorbs them quite! would steal the thing!
First for themselves, next any other,
Who spinster feelings wish to smother.

But when Pa heard the young man's name,
He did not look the happy same,

But said to Ma, "Oh ! had it been
Some other man had saved our queen !"

" Why ?" said she, with an anxious frown.

Said Pa, " I hear this much down Town :
The man who brought our daughter home,
A smuggler is ! who seas doth roam
In search of contrabanded goods,
Which hides he somewhere in the woods,
Or rocks, near Hastings round about,
Spot we have orders to find out.
Some time before his father died,
From far off have we often spied
Both, with cargo most suspicious
Of drinks, doubtless most delicious !
But where they hide it none can find,
They are so clever with their blind."

(The Coastguard wiped with sleeve his lips,
Which watered at the thought of sips
Of grog, he saw these men possess ;
Wished he had some, truth to confess,

But he was a man ordained by law
To never wink at what he saw.)

" Since his death, I mean the old one's,
Son ' hobnobs ' with doubtful bold ones,
And is their Captain, so I learn,
Who soon I fear will hanging earn.
Jane must not wed him, I forbid
She goes a courting "—

          (But she did !
For no more courting incentive
Is there than Order Preventive ;
Forbidden fruit, oh ! is so sweet,
All steal some, aye, the most discreet,
Though all such deeds such try to gild
With garnished tale of doubtful build,
Much, much better left unsaid, for
In all such tales one sees a flaw)—

" Besides he owns a doubtful craft,
A suspicious looking private raft,
Armed with big cannon fore and aft ;
He and his crew look dangerous set
Lonely mid ocean to be met ;

Dark Tales oft also float about,

The truth of which is not found out

As yet, but will be some fine day,

For 'truth will out' wise people say.

Absent weeks, ay! months together,

It is somewhat doubted, whether

Some merchant-men may not have been

On high seas robbed—ship scuttled clean.

The crew seems always full of money

At each return, which seems but funny

When we to seaman's wage give thought—

Such services are cheaply bought.

In drunken fit one of the crew

Boasted, he certain things well knew

Which, if he openly but told,

Would hang the crew and captain bold,

For worse than murder had been done,

Upon high seas one certain run ;

A Spanish ship laden with gold,

Had been attacked and in blood cold,

The crew butchered, not one was spared

To tell how other shipmates fared.

He further said, in drunken fit,

The plunder rich—his share of it—

Was not enough, that Captain stowed
The bulk away, and none had shewed
The secret spot where hidden treasure
Lay concealed in heaped up measure,
For his, the Captain's, secret pleasure.
A sad thing happened, strange to say,
A few days after that same day,
The drunken sailor thus had said—
He was lifeless found with broken head.
Who did the deed none ever knew ;
It was, some said, one of the crew ;
Others—the Captain did the deed,
To save his treasure for his greed :
But sure it was that man was killed,
For some foul reason blood was spilled."

Said Ma, "You must mistake have made,
Piracy cannot be his trade!
This Richard Glover looks as mild,
A mannered thief as Byron's child,
And speaks as soft as turtle dove—
Surely! with Jane he his in love
Earnestly!—had we not better,
Until more we know, Jane, let her

See him; for may it be not wrong
What ill is said of him by strong
Headed enemies existing,
Who will ever be persisting,
When opportunities arise,
In praising some to downward skies?
No, no, old man, let me alone
Until we both have wiser grown;
If he is rich, you may depend
Vilified is he by some kind friend!
More—Believe I not in smuggler tales
Why! *you* have said not one there sails
That *you* can see about this part
To find out which is *your* sole art.
Besides, if later on we hear,
Rumours that are a little queer,
We soon can end the courting match,
The lover's different ways despatch!"

Remembering well his courting days,
The husband smiled at wife's changed ways;
Mothers forget their early feelings
In all their children's marriage dealings;

That once they may have made reply,

"Part me from him and I shall die!"

Or perhaps they purposely forget

How many lovers they have met

And parted from to whom they vowed,

"With my whole heart thou art endowed,"

Although it may have been oft broken!

Before such dreadful fibs were spoken!

"I tell you what I only heard,

And if you think it is absurd,"

Said Coastguard Man to zealous wife,

"There is an end now to our strife;

I will more nothing have to do

With this affair, but leave to you

To do what you think is the best;

But secret keep from me the rest.

Remember! should I find it out,

That this young man prowls thus about,

My duty is to him arrest,

In prison garb he will be dressed,

And sent away for life the rest,

To linger in a cold stone cell.

Until they ring the prison bell—
Ring Richard Glover's life's death knell;
Ill doers I do not defend,
The gallows is their fitting end.
Perhaps misinformed may I have been,
Remains the sequel to be seen;
Still there never was a rumour yet,
But some foundation you might get."

Like ladies, wife would have last word,
"I think," she said, " you talk absurd;
There never was found foundation
For true mis-representation;
Think how many there are that live,
Who always idle tales will give,
Whose sole delight is to backbite
Sweet innocence with venomed spite."

PART IX.

—o◯o—

Oh ! for the days
Of Duelling ways
When Bullet laid Bully Low !

Bully's strong secure are made !
Once the keen sharp blade
And pistols did
Deeds forbid
Which nought hinders now—
Strongest Bully wins the Row !
For on Strongest ! Biggest ! Gods !
Bestow unfair odds.
Thus taunt, brag they,
In their way
Bravely, but truly
Cowardly Contemptibly !

Oh! for the days
Of duelling ways
When Bullet laid Bully Low!

     *   *   *   *   *

A Rival! now we must create,
Love fiercer burns with Rival hate;
Minus Rivals courting *is* flat,
Awfully insipid and all that;
Some married life say is too tame,
Wants more excitement! such I blame!
The sentiment of but a spark,
Some jilted male who loves deeds dark;
People ought married never be
Who wish for more exciting spree!

   " Like Ballast which the ship carries—
Unsteadily it goes without—
Is the wife whom the man marries—
Men single pitch and toss about;
O'er roughest billows man will glide,
   With virtuous wife to help to steer;
Wife ballasted with love for guide
   No human ship a storm need fear!"

About this time there lived at Battle

Lord Malaprops' Son, Captain Rattle;

Lord Malaprop was Magistrate

County, possessed of large estate;

A jolly old buck in his way,

In youth had been, as Lords are, gay!

Yet one safe point had had at least;

Though he dearly loved the noble beast—

(Polo then was not—liked Tent Peg—

Polo—knocking ponies on the leg,

Which some call cruel, others! no,

Ponies! from pain when struck Pole-oh!!)—

He never betted on horse races,

Called them National Disgraces.

Even once against them wrote a squib,

Which Racing Gents called a d—— fib!—

And kind friends, because he wrote in verse

—Not enviously of course—worse

Oh! not enviously, no! no!

Though once most rudely said he so,

"Go and write ye something better;"

Modesty forbade them write a letter;

But good or bad 1 leave to you

To judge, dear reader, whether true!

"OUR NATIONAL NOBLE SPORT."

Whilst Lady Fashionables of the Land,
A doubtless spotless innocent band,
Gaily ! patronised " the stand,"

I heard, " They're off," " They're off," some cry !
I saw the horses panting fly,
As spur was plied and whip raised high,

I saw the foam on horses hide,
The prints of wales on horses side,
I saw the blood a trickling tide,

I saw the winning horse shoot past
The post, whose Backer hat up cast,
I saw the look of anguish blast

The Loser, and I saw much more—
A sight that made my heart beat sore ;
In the struggle one of the poor

(I heard its vertebra loud crack),
Horses fell, and, sad, broke its back !
The horse was carted from the Track

Instantly, lest pitying thought,
Might spoil our "Noble National Sport,"
So eagerly by nobles sought;

Nor slackened cry " Two to one barr one "
And oaths from almost every tongue
Shouted amid uproarious fun!
Where but the Race of Vice is Run,
Where Vice by villainy is outdone,
Where Money is lost but never won
Honorably—Oh! ennobling sport!
Suppress it by all means we ought,
Of total extinction nor stop short,
Lest in Hell's Coils more may be caught.

And furthermore, when but a child—
(Ay, cursed* with genius was he—

---

* The Curse of Curses—A vacillating mind
   Too active, keen to external surroundings
   By sensitiveness backed, called Thin-Skinned!
   That would, that would not; that dare, that dare not
   Lest it might, or lest it might not, offend;
   That looks this way, that looks that way, that weighs
   And balances so actively beforehand,
   Until profusion of Pro's and Con's ends

Lord M-A-L-A-P-R-O-P—

In that it was checked in the bud

Blessed ! it mostly lands one in the mud,

In the Slough of Mental Despond

Deep, note Byron on critics fond.)—

He drove his Infant Teacher wild,

By variations written long,

Upon an Infant School child's song,

Thus—

> Once there was a little boy,
> With curly hair and pleasing eye,
> Who always, always, told the truth,
> And never, never, told a lie.
> Once there was a little boy,
> With curly hair and pleasing eye,
> Who never, never, told the truth,
> But always, always told a lie.

In Hellish Chaotic Indecision ;
Which to the mind non-sensitive to all ! all !
Serenely indifferent but to self ! self !
The Thick-Skinned can be no more comprehended
Than the pain they inflict, but do not feel
Where they blindly, indifferently tread.
God help the first ! the latter help themselves.

The first grew up to be a man,
  With curly beard and pleasing eye,
But prospered not—such seldom can—
  Because he never told a lie.

The last grew up, and lived long too,
  With curly beard and pleasing eye,
In riches rolled—such mostly do—
  Because he always told a lie.

The one he died and went to heaven,
  The other died and went to—well—
Never mind, we will—cannot say,
  Parsons differed, not one could tell.

(Unfortunately vice succeeds
Too frequently with most men's deeds;
Honesty, however much sought,
Can now for riches scarce be bought;
Why? It its owner scarce repays,
The world has outgrown virtue's ways,
The outward show, paste-jewelled swell—
Hypocrisy doth so excel—
Than diamond rough better tell!

In honesty now few believe,

Each, judged by each, tries to deceive,

So that, inch by inch, 'tis dying,

And few think honesty worth trying !

The few that do scarce bare thanks get—

None ever knew a bankrupt yet

But the bigger the smash he made,

The more respected in that trade.

Two bankruptcies big, and one fire,

A merchant cannot soar much higher ;

One step only then to ascend,

Director become,   Once attend

On the Board, with choice chosen chums.

Eat the cake and pocket the plums

Whilst lawyers liquidate the crumbs.

The safest, best-paying game out,

Much honoured too, there is no doubt ;

Grabbed at by Titles and M.P's,

Who oft sell names for what they please.

If prosecuted—but as a joke—

It always ends in harmless smoke,

Except ! for the shareholders poor !

Widows some—homeless, evermore !

Oh ! shame upon that legislation
That prosecutes not wealth and station ;
Ay ! True, I fear, is that old saw,
" There is for rich and poor a law."
For Directors Fraudulent none
Aiding, Abetting, ill deeds done !
Hard-prosecute, example make,
Nor pity give for safety's sake ;
Mercy to such is sin, mistake,
Or will others follow in their wake !) *

Being kind-hearted, lived had he
In these Bank Holidays of spree—
(Bank Holiday turned into song
Is—" a good intention gone wrong—)
We can imagine that he then,
Might have used his young kindly Pen.
The cruelty to mitigate,
On " donkeys " practised at " that fête "
Something after this style, of course
Better much, and with trebled force—

---

* The bigger the rogue, the larger the smash,
  The lesser the sentence, *vide* Glasgow's crash.

Gipsy Neddy's Prayer—Friendless Forlorn.

Oh ! I won't inform, but you know, Sir,
(Would that somebody did) on the go, Sir,
Ever with a curse and a blow, Sir,

Is no joke; with seldom to stay, Sir,
My stomach a morsel of Hay, Sir—
Sometimes I scarcely can bray, Sir !

Whilst children and people and folks, Sir,
All laughing and cracking their jokes, Sir.
Insist ! upon galloping " mokes " Sir;

Thus blame I not you when I say, Sir,
(Never mind what I secretly pray, Sir)
" Bank Holiday " to me is no play, Sir,
But no fault I'll find,
Be only but kind,
Will it rain, do you think, to-day, Sir?

Replied the scoundrel to his Ass,
His words I would not by let pass,
" Gee up, Damn ye, gee up." Alas !

Och! murther! dont hit my poor head! Sir,
It makes my poor heart feel like lead! Sir,
Is it wicked to wish oneself dead, Sir?

Oh, dear! oh, dear! my poor back! Sir,
And sides! which you constantly whack! Sir,
And bones sore! which almost you crack! Sir,

Oh! don't hit me there, if you please! Sir,
God! you've blinded me!!! and my knees, Sir,
From birth, which never knew ease, Sir,

Ache! tremble! shake! none too strong! Sir,
For heavy! are some of the throng! Sir;
Oh! don't use a stick quite so long! Sir.
But no fault I'll find,
Be only but kind,
Don't you think donkey-riding is wrong, Sir?

Replied the scoundrel to his ass,
His words I would not by let pass,
" Gee up, Damn ye, gee up." Alas!

Night long delayed,
Thus Neddy prayed:

" *Thank God the day is done,*
With eye smashed ! sightless one !
Please God to-morrow's sun
May never rise ; rain ! hail !
Thunder ! lightning ! without fail !
Descend ! all pleasures blind !
Through life but kicks and cuffs I find,
Why made ye God man so unkind ? "

To Malaprop's son now return,
His heart with Rival love make burn.
Rattle was tall, five feet eleven,
Handsome, of course, just thirty-seven ;
A Captain in the Royal Household,
Bedecked with sword and lace of gold ;
He was of such who knew Town well,
A Man on Town ! a Heavy Swell,
Who thought his heart by little Cupid,
Impregnable—how very stupid !—

There is no heart of either sex,
But Cupid can at will perplex,

For Venus and Cupid work as one,
Combine in all things to be done ;
Cupid harasseth maiden thought,
With male heart then doth Venus sport ;
Thus when Love's arrow from bow parts
It always joins two loving hearts.

Yet Cupid has a rival passion,
Assuming often Cupid's fashion :
But Passion is another thing,
Abominates a wedding ring ;
The difference easily perceive,
One marriage means, one to make grieve ;
Then honour render Cupid's bow !
And arrow when dart strikes true blow !

Thus young and old may sing these lines,
When for a heart a heart sore pines—
Haste thee sweet Cupid, bow and dart,
Pierce me and—you know—through the heart ;
But lest the wound should leave a sting,
Send with thy dart a wedding ring,
With which fast wed, and may we never,
In wish or deed or true love sever.

Captain Rattle was one day sent,

By Malaprop, of course he went,

With Orders to the Coastguard man,

Jane's father, whom he told to scan

The seas, and keep a sharp look out,

To see if smugglers prowled about.

For, said he, " Pa, Lord Malaprop,

Hath orders had such deeds to stop ;

Hath been advised there doth abound,

Smuggling somewhere the coast around."

Before he left, Miss Jane he saw,

In mind the Captain said, " Haw ! haw ! "

Bah ! Jove ! what deuc-ed tempting toy,

For wicked, naughty, loving boy !

And then he said to ma, aloud ;

" You doubtless are of daughter proud,

True chip ma'am of the parent stock

(Half had, he said—of the old block)

Doubtless, madam, at that same age,

You were as pretty—quite the rage."

On Love, no fool was Captain Rattle,

Knew he well how flattery's prattle

Would please mamma ; he knew he ought,
To win the daughter, ma, first court ;
Knew Love's battle is half obtained,
When ma and pa's consent is gained.

No sooner had the Captain gone,
Than ma began comment upon
His words, and looks, said, " It was plain,
He sheep's eyes cast at daughter Jane."

"But, ma," said Jane, "Just think of Richard,
Knew he, would he not feel *wretched*—"
(Oh, pray laugh not, I am no poet,
A rhymster poor, and I know it)—

" Pooh ! Richard," she said, with look of scorn
" Who's he, compared with this lord born ?
Richard be blowed, should my lord ask,
Performance of the wedding task ;
D'ye think I'd let yer marry he,
If a lord 'ud make yer his la-dee ?
Mind, you girl, should he call once more,
Quick open for him the front door ;

Do all you can to try to please,

The captain pray set at his ease.

Poor Jane began to shed hot tears,

For Richard now she had some fears ;

She loved him dearly, (so she thought,)

Of sweethearts second now thought nought.

One year imagine quick had passed,

Since of the two we wrote the last ;

When Jane in Dripping Well took dive,

Was fished therefrom but half alive ;

During which time they had met often,

Until towards each, each heart did soften

Like new putty, but which, grown old,

Hardens like heart, with love grown cold.

They met in sunshine and in rain,

They parted oft to meet again,

Only fresh vows to re-renew,

More loving they each time both grew.

Both sighed and loved the more intense,

As Jane's papa made fresh pretence,

This courtship sternly to oppose,

Would none of it as reader knows.

His calls the Captain oft renewed,
In heart he secretly Jane sued ;
Of course he always made excuse
Of such sort, " Smuggling was abuse
Of the worst sort he ever saw
Or knew of breaking sacred law,"
And, " that he came but just to hear,
If smugglers had been seen there near."

Ma often left the two at home,
From both she slyly oft did roam ;
The Captain guessed then how things stood,
Thought he might do just as he would ;
But found it was no earthly use,
To hint at wrong, try right seduce ;
The more and more persisted he,
The more and more resisted she ;
At first he only meant flirtation,
It ended in heart resignation,
As such things usually do,
Which surpriseth not, I dare say too.
Though of " mésalliance " he had dread,
Yet as time passed with constant tread,

So love increased, and birth pride fled
And—right—you guess the rest—he asked Jane wed.

Said Jane, " You, Sir, much honour me,
But, truth to tell, I am not free."
" Not free ! " said he, much in surprise,
" Oh ! hang it," thought, then in her eyes
Looked lovingly, sighed, squeezed her hand,
Then placed his arm round her waistband ;
Soft nearer towards him gently drew,
For, artful bird, he full well knew,
Gently does it—wins in the end—
Will ladies' " no " to " yes " oft bend.
He did not rave and make pretence,
That suicide he would commence,
But softly drew, until he pressed
The maiden to his manly breast ;
And, when some little time had sped,
In loving whispers to her said :
" But if you were, what would you say,
Answer, darling, Yes ! Yes ! I pray ! "

She made no answer, gave a blush,
As if she wished some thought to crush :

For, truth to tell, the more she saw,

Her lover new she liked him more.

Though Jane was born in humble sphere,

She loved a polished man more dear,

Or dearly, than uneducated

Boorish Roughs—such men she hated.

Now Richard Glover was not polished,

In all his sayings he abolished,

Those loving little nothings all,

That tickle maidens short and tall.

Wavered now Jane, in love once true,

Stronger, as thought to elsewhere flew ;

And by his polished tittle-tattle,

She got to liking Captain Rattle,

The future Lord of Battle

Abbey, much, much, much too fond,

For one engaged by wedlock's bond

Of promise—naughty, fickle girl—

Just like them though, away they hurl

Poor unfortunate number one,

When richer ones thereafter run,

(The standing joke ladies forgive,

Minus poking fun men could not live).

PART X.

—o◯o—

Peace! Slumber not in Sure Security,
Thou wilt never reign in futurity
Universal.   This is a World of Strife,
Wars ever were, and ever will be rife
Whilst Ambition lives.   War is but the trade
Of foul Ambition by Rogues and Kings made;
Ambition lives alway, goading to war,
And Ambition for Rank ever struggles—nor
Can even Christianity War avert,
Ambition inherent will ever assert.
Then what hopes have Nations Peace shall reign supreme?
None!   Universal Peace is but a Dream!
Oh! Mentor, instinct tells me thou art right,
Advise me Mentor, Peace likes not to Fight!
Then hearken, Peace; There are but Three Stages
In all the histories of the ages

Of all nations ; First, Struggles to achieve ;
Ambition assuaged, this will in time leave,
After conquest, boastful power, indolence,
Dangerous luxury, carelessness ; Thence
Back to first imbecility it tends,
Unless to watchfulness Peace ever bends ;
For might neglected, oft migrates to sway,
Thus nations have had, and will have, their day.
Slumber ! and Ambition will soon encroach,
Then prepared be Peace to Fight War's approach ;
For thou art Part Paradox, Reignst by Might,
Ambition made Heaven Hell's Dire Majesty Fight.

＊　　　＊　　　＊　　　＊　　　＊

Now let us go to Battle Abbey,
(The ride to which is rather shabby
Picturesquely—in truth the scene
All round about *is* rather mean),
For Captain Rattle then dwelt there,
And Lord Malaprop—his revered père.

First, the ancient Church has been restored.
With painted tiles has been re-floored,

Repaired within, new roofed without,
Rebuilt again, without a doubt ;
Like knife with handle new, and blade,
Original once, again thus made ;
Close shaved of all things ancient clean
Has this once old, now new, church been ;
Antiquarians raving setting,
Meddlings (Parson) much regretting.

The Abbey gates stand near close by,
From church a stone's throw (very nigh),
Through which the Abbey may be seen,
Above the Abbey's archway screen ;
Which archway is a noble pile
Of stone and mortar, brick and tile.

The Abbey is an olden building,
Inside resplendent with bright gilding :
Was built in days of Monks of old.
By Norman Monks with Saxon Gold.
William the Conqueror made a vow,
That if he won that little row,
T'wixt him and Harold, Saxon king,
He there stone masons then would bring,

Build a *Monkry* on the spot,
In memory of the victory got.

That victory he won all know,
English History tells us so;
There called The Battle of Hastings.
Should have been Battle of Bastings—
Stay, the Battle of " Battle" it ought
Be called, where these two armies fought,
For, before that battle did commence,
There was no place called Battlo; hence
Thence " Battlo" named, that very spot,
Where Normans Saxons gave it hot.

William the Conqueror's Hosts landed,
Where, of course, his vessels stranded,
In Pevensey Bay, to the right
Of Hastings, towards the Isle of Wight,
Or, more correctly, Bulverhide,
From Hastings just a two mile ride,
Through St. Leonards, Warrior Square,
Peaceful, fashionable quarter there.

William and Harold were related,
Somewhat remotely, it is stated ;
Themselves upon terms friendly placed,
Each other in their arms embraced
Whene'er they met—when they parted
They seemed like friends broken-hearted.

But William was the much more clever
Of the two, by far.   Whenever
He, Harold, went and stayed with him,
William, then Duke, but played with him ;
And when Harold was top heavy,
Drunken promises would levy.

Duke William had some barren land
In Normandy, half chalk, half sand :
One day he said to Harold, " Cousin,
Give I you this for yards a dozen,
Of British soil, or British land,
On Britain's Isle, upon the strand,
Or what with just an Old Bull's hide.
I land can cover by sea side."

" Done," said Harold, it looked a lot,
He thought he had best bargain got.

Then Wily William had deeds made
Of this said bargain, so some said;
Then orders gave to well beat out
An old bull's hide, to cover about
As much of land as well would hold
His army brave, of robbers bold.
Thus gained he right to thus much land,
As well would hold his Norman band;
Thus Harold was by law bond bound
To let him land upon this ground
Unopposed; thus Duke William gained
A footing here which he maintained.

As daily passed Times constant tide,
This spot they nicknamed " Bulverhide ; "
As named they that so named they " Battle,"
Where swords on armour once did rattle.

They did not then make quite that noise
We now do with our warlike toys
Of Woolwich Infants, of eighty tons ;
Martini-Henry and Gatling guns.
Since then, in weapons what a change :
We now command a ten mile range

Direct ten miles send to the spot,

From gun a nearly two-ton shot.

Torpedoes introduce we too,

(What next I wonder shall we do)

A sort of underhanded trick

Of war, well worthy of old Nick

The Devil.

Advanced we in Christianity

Thus, blessed would be humanity ;

Humanity ! doth such thing exist,

When nations still in war persist !

Civilization ! what a dream !

When brutality reigns supreme.

Before William were bloody wars,

After William the same horrors

Occurred, it seems they ever will ;

Yet we assert that up the hill

Of improvement we daily go !

We ought to, as the more we know :

The more we know, the less excuse

For war, of knowledge but abuse,

To settle quarrels of no use !

State Religion—Pooh! there is none!

Or wars would never be begun

Yet oft do Czars and Kings and men

For sake of God war now and then.

Following God's command to Moses, (?)

" Go smash ye other nations' noses "

(Though I think not God so did give

Orders to kill those He made live ;

No God of Love would counsel war,

Love ye your neighbour is God's Law.

But of the Abbey let me talk ;

From promise William tried to walk,

Until some monk did him remind

In fulfilling it he was behind,—

Worried him, no doubt, poor devil,

Out of temper's usual level,

Until he got The Royal Consent,

For stone and mortar, bricks, cement.

Thus Monks of Old, like Priests of Young,

Persuasive were with smooth oil'd tongue,

But woe to them who promise gave,

And after wished the same to save !

Hell Fire (no treacle) and Brimstone
Would ever at their heads be thrown.
Yes, Priests of yore were foxy boys,
To pick purse-pocket for heaven's joys.

The Abbey built in went this Monk,
With close-shaved face and portly trunk,
(Grown portly on the Port oft drunk)
Which he and Order made their quarters ;
Therein forbidding Eve's fair daughters ;
For Frisky Monk and Sprightly Nun
Indulgeth not in usual fun
Convincing thereby every one,
What sin it is to have a son
Yet had their parents kept asunder,
From whence would both have come, I wonder ?
Yea ! Priests and Nuns would have been never
Had Ma's and Pa's kept single ever.

Having stated why this place was built
(In palliation for blood spilt)
Skip we what passed there in meantime—
Dark deeds more wicked than sublime—

To Civilization return
Of later ages, there thus learn—
    "Though imperfect still in many things
    Priests, Parsons, Bishops, Queens, and Kings
    Are more enlightened, and we are
    Individually bettered far.
    Then off with hats, it might have been
    Heads of yore, now, God save our Queen :
    Yes, Britons now may well feel proud,
    They are with mother queen endowed.
    Who could with such a Ruler Royal
    (Who rules by love love's fettered soil)
    Ever harbour thought disloyal—
            Ay, God save our Queen ;
            For ever has she been
            Our mother !
            More watchful or kind
            Never shall we find
            Another !

PART XI.

—o◯o—

In Memoriam of—
Crisp Christmas ! Season of Mistletoe,
Holly, Yule Logs, Snap-Dragons aglow,
Plum Puddings, Mince Pies, Fun, Jollity,
Charades, Quadrilles. Young Frivolity,
Rounds of Visits 'midst decorations,
Children, Sweethearts, Friends and Relations,
Thus seemed it long ago !
Not seems it so
Now ! as in our youth !
Then ! then ! seemed in truth,
Christmas Day, Christmas Time, most jolly—
Thought melancholy !
Mirth is called folly,
Old age youth now feigns,
Young youth mirth disdains,
Precocity reigns ! Past seems all Play !

Youth now is agod, old,

Young love is so cold,

For wealth is all sold ;

Loved ones have married,

Wealth hath not tarried,

Vows have miscarried ;

Ambition flattered

False—Bright hopes shattered,

Dear friends have scattered,

And,

And, Old Christmasses ! have passed away !

Not now as it did ! seems Christmas Day ! —

Ah ! me, the Past !

Or, or is it, that youth having flown

And Riches, envious I have grown,

Spending alone my Christmas, slighted

By Welcome Past Guests oft invited ?—

Ah, me, the Past !

In her carriage sat she, driven fast,—

Yes ! yes ! she saw me—when met we last ?

Rich ! I wooed her ! almost did win her !

But stepped there forth a Richer Sinner,

And now to-day, Christmas Day ! lonely !
And only ! but
Pork !—goose nor apple-sauce for dinner !
Ah ! me ! the Past !

*   *   *   *   *

The night was dark, the wind blew strong,
No better time for deeds of wrong
Often occurred.   The snow and sleet
Earth covering as in winding sheet,
Against all things rough rudely beat,
Indoor made outdoor life retreat.
The Angry Gale in gusts loud growled,
Amidst the rocks and crags fierce howled,
Like hosts of devils in fiendish glee
Of subterranean mystery.
The surf ran high, made dangerous shore
For harbour bound tired sailor poor :
The thunder rolled, the thunder clashed,
As vivid flames of lightning flashed,
Then headlong rushed from zigzag track,
Night making hellish hideous black !
Midnight crept o'er, ay, still more dark !
And—dead silence reigned—nor watch dog's- Hark !--

What noise was that ?   Oh, God ! a cry
For help ! I heard despairingly ;
Listen ! it calls again, quite clear,
As if a struggle for life dear
Hard wrestled on, O Lord, quite near !
List—List ! again—Far from the shore—
Now high in air above once more
Is same unearthly noise repeated—
What can it be ?—blood overheated ?—
Hark ! there it is—repeats itself—
Of earth is it ? or is it elf ?
Or do I make a fool of self ?—
My knees they tremble, I am bereft
Of once bold heart with fear twain cleft,
My daylight courage hath me left,
Or, should I easily recognize,
I hear but seagulls' night storm cries.

　　*   *   *   *   *

Darker and darker grew the dark,
When lo ! there shone a brigh blue spark ;
T'was coastguard signal for the fight,
Smugglers expected had been that night,
(How suspected we know not quite)

And preparations made complete,
This time the smugglers to defeat.

It was a battle on small scale,
Thick all around, like stones of hail,
Blows fell heavily ; pistol shots
Exchanged were, leaving blood-red spots
Where bullet entered breast or head.
Some wounding, others killing *dead*—
So much for powder and vile lead.

Attack well planned, quite overpowered,
For justice now the prisoners cowered :
But Richard Glover ! where was he ?
More than the rest he fought bravely.
Jane's father ! did he take a part
Against his daughter's own sweetheart ?

Each in the dark, each met and fought.
Thrusted and parried as they ought,
When from their swords bright sparks their flew.
By sight of which both each well knew.
" Hold ! Richard, hold ! " said the old man.
" Run for your life, boy "—Richard ran,

When up came a coastguard brother,

Mistook the old man for another,

Laid on his sword, engaged with him,

A duel hot fierce waged with him.

The combat Richard heard commence,

To save Jane's pa returned he thence,

Just, just in time to parry blow

That would have laid the old man low.

He saved the old man, but alas !

A man with sword and hilt of brass

Poor Richard struck, who fell as dead,

Though only stunned upon the head.

(Near where the Aquarium (?) now stands,

Was fought this battle on the sands

Against these smuggler bold brigands)

In solitary cell, with bread,

Cold water, and bare floor for bed,

Was Captain Richard Glover found,

With handcuffs on, leg iron-bound.

Upon a rude stone bench or seat,

He sat and thought.   His heart hard beat,

Thinking what sentence would be given,

How long from Jane he would be driven ;

Henceforward determined reform,

Like all men when caught in a storm,

Or fall sick, then, like the old gent,

Pray, if they think life will be spent,

But recovered, forget their vow,

Commence life again anyhow—

" The Devil fell sick, a saint would be ;

Got well, the devil a saint was he."

But long had Richard rued the time

He turned from path of right sublime ;

It stopped his wedding—Jane's father

Than a smuggler, would have rather

She married a sooty chimney sweep,

Howe'er for Dick she much might weep ;

Would not admit nor excuse make,

Smuggling was but a bad mistake.

But *we* know well that cask of brandy

Fate made to float by much too handy,

His father's craft in by-gone days,

Influencing Dick's later ways

Though (too late) repentant now he growled,
"Cursed be that cask which towards us bowled."
(Temptation indulged however small
Ends mostly in one's sure downfall).

Yet Dick felt more cheerful than sad,
In truth, he now felt somewhat glad.
Glad that he had Jane's father saved,
Glad thus her father had behaved
Towards him, bid him run away,
Which shewed in heart no malice lay—
A ray of hope for better day.

Yet a more important matter
As cheerful made him as this latter;
In the smuggling trade, with long blue beard.
Richard had had a partner feared,
Now dead, vanquished in the late fight.
Leaving Richard thus master quite
Of secret, where the hidden gold
Lay piled in heaps, and heaps untold.
Richard to Bluebeard had been cat's paw,
For his it was whose word was first law;

Poor Richard, he but played the Second
Fiddle, though had first been reckoned
Till now, no doubt, in this, my tale,
To read through which I hope will fail
None—recommend it to your friends—
Further editions are author's ends.

Richard had gone about in fear
Of life and limb, lest Bluebeard, near,
Should knife him ; lest he, Richard, might
Let secret out he wished kept tight.
Relief it was to Richard's mind—
Not now could dreaded Bluebeard find
Opportunity to Richard kill
Whene'er it suited Bluebeard's will.

MORAL—Dark deeds in partner life
Are deeds which cut like two-edged knife.

PART XII.

Load, present, fire, right-about-face,
Quick march boys, redouble your pace,
Halt, turn, steady boys, steady,
Once more boys, once more, ready,
Present, fire, Aim boys at their head,
Kill the devils red!
Now fly to the Caves! to the Caves!
All cry, to the Caves! to the Caves!
Shoulder to shoulder stand by,
For life his hardest each try,
Fierce fight we or die, in the Caves,
Our Stronghold or graves!

* * * * *

Groping along on hands and knees,
They stopped sometimes their limbs to ease

Of burthen, Gold, bright Gold, again—
Words of magic that in Tales reign
Of robbers supreme.

Weird Caverns
Dark are Smugglers Private Taverns ;
For evil doers, fit abodes,
Towards which leadeth secret roads
And winding paths, cunningly hidden,
Entrance thereto strictly forbidden
To all who know not magic word
Of Countersign, at Challenge heard.
'Neath that Hill where you Castle stands,
Caverns exist, where brigand bands
Of Ruffians once did lawless trade,
Who heaps of Stolen Gold there laid,
(Grand find for some Excursion Blade).
These Caverns lie in deep, deep earth,
Buried from whence no sound of mirth
Can be heard without.   Dread Earthquake
Made them, which once the world did shake,
Make tremble, as in convulsive throes
Of death, for why, God only knows.
Rocks upon Rocks of Tons and Tons
Tumultous fell, with noise of guns,

Multiplied by Omnipotence,

Guided by God's all Prescience.

Who first found them none now can tell,

But in these Caves there was deep well

Where, doubtless, victims had been thrown,

Who, doubtless, there gave life's death groan,

A mangled mass of flesh and bone.

To Battle Abbey, once there led,

A pathway underground, some said,

Where many a cask of goodly Port

Sent there had been, well known not bought.

The Monks of old, a doubtful set,

As in a day's march could be met,

Spiritual absolution gave

For Casks of Spirits from this Cave,

Saved Souls and Silver at one go,

Thus two birds killing at one throw.

Richard and Bluebeard groped their way

In Subterranean Passage—" Stay !

What noise was that," Bluebeard enquired,

" So help me heaven," he said, " All fired,"

(Vide Yankee Dictionary) "but stop!
This bullet in your skull I'll pop,
False if I find you, my young friend,
I'll instantly your young life end."

Richard trembled ; they were alone,
None could have heard his dying moan ;
He could have stabbed, of course, Bluebeard,
But murder such his Conscience feared ;
Although the stronger of the two,
All killing he abhorred to do ;
At fisticuffs no better hand,
On any nose could straightly land,
Back heel, Cross buttock, quickly floor,
Such men as Bluebeard, two or more ;
But with the knife had no compassion,
With horror thought of an Assassin.

Through winding passage into Hall,
Supported by thick columns tall,
(Where has been held a Royal Ball),
They came, struck light, then looked around,
But heard not living mortal sound ;

No sound of any sort was heard,
Save these two men no shadow stirred.
No trickling water from the roof
Even (these Caves are dry and waterproof,,
Though o'er the soul there seemed to creep
The dreaded jump. the dreaded leap
Of ghostly ghost from vasty deep.

Weird looked this Hall by candle light,
Full swallowed in the darkness quite,
It oppressive was. and it seemed
Like Pit of which John Bunyan dreamed,
With fancied dancing imps and devils,
Indulging in fantastic revels.

There radiated from this place.
Or Hall, more Passages   To space
Infernal all. they seemed to tend,
Winding in a tortuous bend.
There Stranger would. at life's dear cost,
Wander alone there until lost.
In Roof there was a widened cleft,
As Nature there the rocks had left

In Chaos.   Up through this same crack,
Standing on Richard's inclined back,
Bluebeard self-hoisted.   Then was seen
Another Hall, where piled had been
All Bluebeard's ill-got golden gains,
At cost of blood and scattered brains.

There Richard tracked him one dark night,
There he and Bluebeard had had fight,
There Bluebeard " caved in " to stronger might,
There promised half the fortune quite
If Richard would keep secret tight ;
Richard replied, " agreed, all right!"
To vanquished Bluebeard's chagrined delight,
And now comes welcome, welcome sight,
My bed-room candle burning bright,
Or brightly—which ever is best—
A few words more, and then to rest.

Richard, the Smuggler, still there lives,
Exists on what the stranger gives,
Exhibits round the weird old place,
Nor thinks his past deeds a disgrace.

His tale with mine does not agree
Exactly, betwixt you and *me*,
But there, I see not how it should,
Fiction is fibbing well understood.
But tale fast bring we to a close,
Much must be left, you may suppose,
Describing, in so short a space,
Hastings—Lively Watering Place.

P.S.—To fiddle and torchlight
They dance now in these caves at night,
Where you may wander now at large—
Sixpence admission is the charge.
Joking apart, these caves repay
A visit well for such outlay.

PART XIII.

—:o:—

Oh ! dance, could I dance, the whole livelong night ;
Then dance away, dance, until morning light ;
One, two, three count, for waltzing and whirling,
Twisting, twining, and gracefully curling ;
One, two, count, for the deuxtemps, the stately,
For this dance is danced courtly, sedately ;
One, two, three count—make a short, sudden stop—
Four—twice twirl—repeat, for the schottishe hop ;
Count one, two, three, four, in equal measure,
Then polka will ye with ease and pleasure ;
Walk modestly through the pleasing quadrille ;
But rush at the gallop just as ye will ;
Languidly lean on the favoured one's arm,
Till thy young beating heart gets somewhat calm ;
Then, when it regains its usual beat,

Ere soul is absorbed again in the feat,
Take champagne for supper, nor sham to eat.

*   *   *   *   *

In Battle Abbey's Banquet Hall,
My Lord there gave a grand state Ball,
Same night that smugglers all were caught,
Same night that Coastguard bravely fought.
Whilst pistol shots rang out death knells,
Indulged the loveliest of 'belles'
In *sparkling*, *brilliant* flirtation,
And Coup-d'Œil insinuation.

Captain Rattle, the son and heir,
Moved listlessly but here and there;
Thought little of the fairest guest
Who would have wedded and made blest
Man of her choice; but girls are allowed
Choice *not* amongst the high-born proud,
Of Life Partner—money decides
Fitting bridegrooms for fitting brides.

Lord Malaprop was first to lead
The ball off grand—he did the deed
With Princess Royal of Timbuctoo,
Whose husband danced in buckled shoe—
Who gave his legs a royal shake,
Then compliment or two did make
To Portly Partner, Lady M——,
Who flattered felt on hearing them.

The Captain, glumpy, "mouched" around,
No charm for him, the merry sound
Of viol, drum, horn and fiddle,
Not danced he up and down the middle,
(Called dancing—mark the quotation—
"Toe and leg intoxication.")
For Cupid had shot him in the heart,
And there he felt the keen wound smart.

But Cupid had for high-born dame
The Captain's heart not set on flame ;
All high-born dames he could not bear,
He liked not well their haughty stare ;
Called ladies of nobility
" Educated effrontery."

His thoughts meandered towards his Jane,
He wished to see her much again,
Although but just the night before,
He saw her safely to her door;—
Innocence he more than thought her
Because she was a poor man's daughter.

Mamas tried useless hard to coax,
With loveliest daughter him to hoax;
The future young Lord M—— was proof,
From each fair prize he held aloof;
He was a fool, of course, such chance
Would make most men with pleasure dance;
Ladies Born. well educated,
Should never be underrated,
Money, title, education,
Beats poor girl wife speculation
Hollow.

But Cupid's shots are made so funny,
No thought He gives to rank or money,
He sends his little dart from bow,
Nor looks for mark, nor high nor low;

And when he sends the dart right home,

Quickly away doth reason roam ;

T'is Cupid's Art, to lovers blind

To faults which others quickly find.

A plan the Captain framed in mind,

Bold, something after such a kind :

Give I Jane's father and her mother,

The portion of a younger brother ;

Send both away and none shall know

Where this old couple after go ;

Send Jane to school, a lady make

Of her, for wife then Jane will take ;

Leave Abbey to a Steward's charge,

Then in my yacht far roam at large ;

What care I what the world may say,

A Lord may do just as he may ;

Hem ! Take a doctor for the wife,

To guard against mishaps to life.

Hah! Speaking of Doctors, up crop
Thoughts terrible two ; Let us pop
Them on paper, Writing in Rhyme,
Measure—Ramble-tonia-Time.

Dense with fogs at their height,
On a drizzly wet night,
Dank slushy sleet raining,
Out-door courage draining,
   Sat slipper shod Doctor Magee ;

Before the fire roasting,
Chilled feet and toes toasting,
His rounds but just ended,
Last poor patient tended,
   Half dozing there cosy sat he ;

A glass of grog sipping,
The night had been nipping,
Which deserved he right well,
As a many could tell
   Of the poor, how kind had he been ;

For he served all the same,

Hoped he gaining thus fame,

The wealthy, noble, poor,

The last less, neither more,

   Except foes them charging less keen.

Drank, took he the Candle-

Stick, as we that handle ;

To bed he up toddled,

Where Madame lay coddled,

   In blankets all downy and warm,

Then quickly undressing,

His form was soon pressing,

Midst feathers and pillows ;

Whilst outside the billows,

   Of wind rough told loud of the storm.

Hard having been plodding,

He soon went off nodding,

As next moment seeming,

He then fell a-dreaming—

   What dreamed he here need I not tell ;

But, not lasted dream long,
When there came a loud strong—
As 'twere in a passion—
Ring, Smashin', and Clashin';
  A ring, loud, from the door night bell,

Roused, he quickly awoke,
Through night tube thus spoke :
" Who is there in such fright,
At this hour of mid-night " ;
  Some drunken joke hoped it might be,

Quick back came reply, " Sir,
Make haste or she'll die, Sir,
My poor wife is dying ;
Oh ! God," said voice crying,
  " Make haste and accompany me."

He quickly descended,
And with the man wended,
Nor asking nor heeding,
Though stranger 'twas pleading,
  As elsewhere had oft gone before ;

Through alley and turning,
Nor doubting—quite spurning,
Of treachery foul, base,
To save life did he race,
But—*he never was heard of more*

His poor wife, alas !
To her now repass.

A life as pure as mortal here could lead,
Had led she, yet Fate thus made her heartstrings bleed;
Poor woman ! poor woman ! words could not tell,
The agony she suffered ere full well
Hope fled ; ere she, his loving, loving wife,
Of seeing him once more despaired in life.
Like some cloud ominous dark hanging o'er
Boding some storm rough just coming before,
So hung there a mental cloud foreshading
Some ill, burthensome-like overlading ;
It seemed to press her down, down, always down ;
Like an evil spell settled there a frown
Expectant, which ever on her brow thence hung,
Quick aged tho woman who was still yet young ;

For, scarce five-and-twenty years had passed o'er
Her, and but five years back she crossed the door
Paternal, to be wed.   Soon turned she grey,
On mind her sad misfortune so did prey ;
It seemed to her that Providence had dealt
Most harshly, at least so she ever felt
When kneeled she down, with hardened heart, to pray,
Soft once, ere Fate had spirited away.
Had he but died—she shuddered at the thought
And crushed it—tried her hardest to—but nought
Yea nought could crush it—forgive her, forgive,
Yes Dead ! she would he were than thus uncertain live
In years of hopeless hope—No, No—repented
She that wish, as loving heart relented,
Only to pray for, in the same short breath,
Heaven's Boon to suffering living kind—Death ;
Ay ! to her, Madness would have been relief,
The Sane most suffer, trial o'erwhelmed with grief ;
Hers, hard, perforce she struggled with and bore,
A widowhood uncertain hanging o'er—
(Hopeful expectation ! hoping ever !
Hopeless uncertainty ! coming never !)—
Until some power pitied, seemingly unkind !
But kind !   drove the poor creature out of her mind.

PART XIV.

—:o:—

Killed in Dread Battle, left alone,
    Soon after we were wed,
By a Soldier to the Altar,
    I yielding young was led ;
The child I carry, weak and wan,
    Was born not when he died,
Oh ! God, that He and I and It
    Were buried side by side.

Pensionless, homeless, friendless, quite,
    1 wish I were not !
Hungry, fainting, famished, craving,
    Fast sinking I wot !

By law-armed-bailiffs rough-ousted,
    Weak—desperate I feel!
Without a penny in the world
    Oh! God, may I steal!

*   *   *   *   *

Lord Malaprop in petty state,
Next morning sat as magistrate,
With local Parson, landed Squire,
Who settled things to their desire.

Did a lean hungry half-starved tramp
A turnip take, "You hardened scamp,"
They all would say with deep surprise,
" Believe we not your self-made lies,
However hungry you might be,
From stealing you ought keep hands free,
Two months' treadmill or two pounds fine,"
Grand choice for those without a *coin*.

Did any poor man shoot a hare,
They then at all with transfixed stare,

Of horror would look, as if God made
Game-dealing his especial trade,
And kept the sport of killing for,
Especial favourites of the law.

Did some poor creature gather sticks
To make a fire on hearth of bricks,
To warm the frozen half-starved thing,
Almost an action they would bring,
These Petty Magistrates, oh ! shame,
To prove the creature was to blame.

A fact well known must I here write
Which shows them in their humble light ;—
Because he did not touch his hat
They sent a man to prison for that.

Then hurrah for the magnanimate
J. P. or Country Magistrate!

Lord Malaprop now took the chair,
Though he and Son came seldom there ;

But, smugglers having been arrested,

The sitting this time was invested

With more than interest of daily ;—

The trying smugglers for Old Bailey,

There to be sent for final trial,

Of liberty or 'its denial.

Rattle in Magisterial chair,

An embryo Magistrate sat there ;

But Richard was the Observed of all,

He stepped forth briskly at the call

Of his name.   He was in youth's prime,

But not before in his lifetime

Had Malaprop or Rattle Seen

This man ; to them he might have been,

And was, as of the dead.   Neither knew,

That in their veins the same blood through

Coursed ; But betwixt Richard, Rattle,

And the Lord of (Abbey) Battle,

The case stood thus, but—No—Yes—Well—

Though sorry tale it is to tell—

Richard and Rattle were brothers

(Half), each had different mothers.

Thereby hangs tale, it not unfold ;

Such stories are best left untold.

A funny feeling o'er each crept
Unconsciously, and there it left
Its mark, quite indefinitely ;
Yet ever affected the three
In dreamland, where especially
Each would the other often see.

PART XV.

—:o:—

In vain did Æsop try to find
An honest man ;
Nor could nor can—
(For honesty is to the mind
Comparative—
Conscience doth give
But elasticity thereto)
Any.   We by long custom do
So soft approach,
Gently encroach,
Each upon our better nature,
That seldom guage we the stature
Of each our deeds ;
Simply our needs,

Or, rather, wishes, regulate.

Honesty, so called, thus I state,

Existeth not—

(And God I wot

Never once intended it should,

Were man's mind by nature all good,

Gauged could not be

Depravity)—

But comparative.   Thus with all ;

Nor regret we,

Nor need fret we,

Did she, we rise through Eve's blessed fall.

    *   *   *   *   *

Six weeks after—How time doth fly !—

The Sword of Justice hung on high

O'er the Judges seat.   Austerely

The Judges Three all looked around,

Whilst heard was not a single sound.

Truth-twisting Barristers looked learned,

As if by study they had earned

Distinction over other men ;

Whilst Reporters sat with ready pen,

Sentence to note on Richard Glover,

The Smuggler and Devoted Lover.

Nor hand, nor foot, nor body stirred,

All round the room was plainly heard

The ticking of the large round clock,

Whilst Prisoner stood in Prisoner's Dock,

Waiting dread Sentence.

                Then Judge said—

First Black Cap fitting on his head,

" Prisoner, Sentence of this Court

Is, Thy young life be Cut thus Short ;

Thou shalt from here be taken hence,

From whence thou shalt be taken thence

To Scaffold, there by neck be hung

Till dead, and after, when unstrung,

Be buried in Jail's Common hole

Or Grave—Lord have mercy on thy Soul."

A shriek ran piercing through the Court,

A woman fainted at the thought,

Of horrid death by Judge decreed,

Or man by man from this world freed.

Poor Jane had heard pronounced the Doom

Of Justice in that awful room ;

Fainting, unconscious, taken to bed,
For weeks she never raised her head;
When Consciousness again returned,
Sentence of Death, she then first learned
Had been respited; but, worse still,
Aye worse than death—upon treadmill
Forty long years substituted
(A stretching of the neck diluted).

Relieved at this Jane gave deep sighs,
Then tears fast trickled from her eyes,
Tears are a woman's great relief,
They sorrow rob of half its grief;
But Broken Hearts' Physician Time
Soon Heart restores to Pristine Prime.

" Hothouse grapes, Mother! Whence came they?"
Asked Jane surprised, yet, truth to say,
She hoped, then guessed, and that quite right,
Then came a feeling of delight
Next moment changed to feeling queer.
At thought of Richard once so dear.
She coloured up at secret thought
"Now Dick is gone, I think I ought

Nevermore think of another,

Well, except *only as a brother*,

No harm in that sure—sure—sure-ly "—

She then again began to cry,

Suddenly she ceased, left off quite,

Then said—and both eyes sparkled bright —

"The Captain is, I must say, kind

Such fruit an invalid to find ;

I wonder, knows he Richard Glover

Was my late—hem !—sweetheart and lover,

Anxious he seems now I am ill,

I ought to thank him, and—*I will*."

PART XVI.

CHURCH.

By Law compel we as we please,
   Unless you send at once Tithe-Rate—
Ask Parson's Pardon on your knees,
   This "Notice" herewith is to state,
The Broker value soon shall seize.

CHAPEL.

The Only True Immaculation,
   Terms, Prompt Cash, Price List of Sittings
   According to their place and fittings
Gratis! Gratis! on application,
Step up, ye sinners, or—D—ation.

ROME.

Unless you worship, First The Pope
Infallible, there is no hope;
   Next, The Virgin (That holy one)—

Less, somewhat, her Son —God least,
To H— you go, shall say the Priest.

MISCELLANEOUS.

Oh ! Terrible Task, where begin ?
The very thought makes brain to spin,
    Hope fall.   Broad Charity to all
Extend ; Would Sect to Sect did the same,
But, Sectarianism knows not the name.

This Chapter may be skipped, and the next,
By all Sensitives of Scripture Text,
And Admirers of Parson Glory—
They interfere not with our Story.

To Bourne from whence none back return,
To tell of what they there may learn,
Under Sentence of Death, Richard lay,
Shortly to be sent—Ah ! which way ?
Divines' advice advised to take,
Divines' Invectives thus he spake,
And thus description of them gave,
Who most will think began to rave —

" I will not have Reverend Pastors

(Reverend, indeed—for what styled ?

Enough to drive a true Saint wild !)

To tell of future life's disasters ;

Who, believed I not what they said,

Would ills predict upon my head.

As specimens of Self Vanity,

Narrow minded Christianity,

Parsons excel all humanity.

As teachers of The Great Above

Mark ye their Brotherly Christian love ;

Like poison they hate another

Non-Sectarian Parson Brother,

And Censure doctrines others teach,

Unfit for Ministers to Preach.

Their Churchyard Christianity note,

Here instances no need to quote,

Refusing the dead, to bury

Unbaptized ! How Christian, very !

So much for Christianity,

Let us peep at their vanity !

Why wear uniform, unless to show

(By laymen satellites affected,

Would be thought Parsons self elected)

They better are than most, or know
More of what is as yet unknown
The Hereafter—such Pride bemoan!
The styling self divinity!
Of self goodness infinity!
Proof! Proof! of Christianity?
No, Vanity! Vanity!
Sublime! sounds the Reverend Brown,
Common! unqualified the noun,
Without the handle placed before
Brown might a Jones be thought next door;
Makes the man, the handle to the name,
Though a woman he may be the same.
Which handle is the Parsons pride,
Or why not outward emblem hide;
Excuse for which cannot be made,
It is but that of Parson Trade,
Advertising, and cheap—aye, much
Like other Tradesmen doing such.
Parsonizing! *T'is but Trade*, I say;
Churches and Chapels, in their way,
But warehouses, where to be sold
Are varied doctrines but for gold;

A few free sittings thrown in cheap,
Attractive lure more gold to reap ;
Where, mark ! contemptible vain youths,
Cudgelling brains for proofs of truths ;
Some but bits of boys
Who preach heaven's joys,
Each and every word
Sounding from such absurd,
In words mock-weighty,
To men of eighty ;
Old saws noting,
Stock phrases quoting ;
For which divine cheek
A phrase let me seek "—

Here paused he a moment as in thought,
Then brightened eyes as he it caught—

" Young ideas scarce yet taken root,
Teaching old ideas how to shoot "
Standing stiff-starched like a poker,
In all their glory vain, of choker ;
Where Curates preach for soles, quite true,
Of slippers—hush—betwixt us two ;

Ministers young, commencing life,

On children up-bringing for a wife,

In full nine sermons out of ten

Obtained, such subjects give up then.

Stay, I must not place Curates bold,

In the Ministerial fold,

Curates will call it ' infra dig.'

Church Chapel treats like lawless prig ;

Ministers can be made of fools,

And Curates too, but then the tools,

The last required for, cost much more,

Universities bar the door.

Quite moneyless no one can be

Made, Doctor of Divinity ;

But any meeting clout can preach,

Even knows he not a word to teach,

So can Church Parson, though this seize—

There are ' like rivers ' P's and P's.

Ah ! I oft wonder what means that cry,

' Called to the cause '—How ? For what ? Whom by ?

As for second call of Minister,

Lies therein thought ought sinister ;

When from loved flock they make a shift,

Knew you one move without a lift

Of salary; Not that I blame

All mortals receiving the same,

But call these "Calls" their proper name,

Such Fibs are Lies, however tame.

Except with those who get no pay

(Itinerent Preachers half cracked,

Ignorance fierce by rabble backed—

Street Spouters disgust, not attract)—

Money! it is! say what you may;

Money! Money! with one and all!

From Archbishop to spouter small!

With Vanity of Choker beside,

Oh! How I hate this Choker Pride,

Making many express disgust!

At Religion! because Parsons must,

Before one's eyesight always thrust

This Coveted Choker, outward crust

Of Self Sanctification; But Hark!

Ye Parson worshippers, and Mark!

What says this Choker?   Here you see

At the most a human D—— D——

With millinery, half a she,
Ticketed Reverend Vanity "—

" Hush ! cease," I said, " such disrespect,"
Continued he, now fiercely erect—

" Parsons but work on the Sixth Sense,
Religion Called, at Man's expense "—

Asked, explain " the Sixth Sense," he gave such kind
Of Description, Proving him out of his mind,—

" Ideas idiosyncratic sheer,
With indefinable feelings not clear,
An indescribable mixture most queer
Of reason, unreason, credulity,
Incredulity, sentiment, hope, fear;
Keen longing for continuation of
Bodily life, ever dear ! ever dear !
Dissolutions dread, not the love for Hence ;
Religious Love of God being but pretence ;
If it were man lived on earth for ever,
·God's disciples would be heard of never ;

Dissolution is man's most dreaded thought,

But for that man would think of God nought ;

'Tis fear of Body, not Soul, troubles mind,

Cowardice through Flesh lest Soul may Torment find ;

Sixth Sense Forming, which is condensed to a breath,

FEAR, Dissolutions Dread, Life shrinking from Death.'

When I asked him, Feared *he* Death ?

"Death ;" said he,

"That staple article of the Stock-in-Trade

Whereon Parsons their pot-hooks crooked hang

And mystify, upon which raving preach they,

Upon which they variations revolve

Most eccentric, because nor provable

Nor contradictory, the one calling,

The end of life, death ; yet, in the sentence next,

Calling that same, the beginning of life

Thereof making a Paradox chaotic ;

Why should I fear it, if by that, you mean,

What is to come ?—I like all else, not knowing !

Even assuming, a Hell deep there be,

Though God Himself in Person Commanded,

If our fore parents were so perfect made

(After the Image of Himself made He man ?

Why thus perfect made by God to unmake ?

Had He *so* made, man could never have fallen

Unless *Satan* than *God* were more subtle—)

Need we, (made after the image of them,

Thus less perfect, that much full lessening

The loftiness of our fall) hopeless be ?

They lost Paradise Once, ay ! perhaps Twice,

For aught History tells, a dozen times,

And Paradise Regained, then why not I ?

Let Death alone, nor speculate, nor fear,

And, seeing it will come when it will come,

Let Death itself its own future provide,

For the heavenly food that man stores up may

Be, after all, for Death's support, lifeless.

Again ask me, Do I fear Death ? I say,

If by that, you mean, The Future, No ! No !

But if, by that, you mean, of The Body,

'Gainst which the good and bad alike grapple,

Evasively wistful, nor successful,

I say "Yes ! above all things Most ! Most ! Most !

(Here felt he his neck where the rope would strangle.)

" Ay, dread ! beyond all ! as doth all living kind,

Or would follow, suicide universal,

Of that, the ordained safeguard."

Oh ! the fearless free-thinking wretch,
Deserved he neck should get a stretch ;
Upon prayer's power to him hinting,
Ideas better imprinting,
Sneeringly sneered he, squinting—

"A Shark and Dolphin, each equally good,
At sea met one day, as such creatures would :
The Dolphin, in fear, immediately turned,
Whilst the shark in pursuit to taste him yearned ;
Each offered up prayer, as we—why not they ?
Think not that mankind but knows how to pray—
Down ! down ! deep dived they then up again,
But fruitlessly, opposite prayers did refrain ;—
'Oh ! Creative Spirit, Grant, Grant I pray,
From this shark's teeth I keep away '—
'Oh ! Creative Spirit, Grant, Grant, I pray,
This Dolphin gets not clean away '—
Twirled, twisted, and doubled each with a will,
But all to no purpose, and thus they do still,
For, as each prayed its hardest, with heartfelt might,
Each got prayer answered ;—thus goes on the flight ;

As men prayed they, each for opposite ends,
Ah! where would all be if to prayer God bends?"

Tale finished, laughed he, then withering said ;—
" Prayer is Blasphemy ! " (turned I quite red ;)
" Knows God what is best for each, every one,
Simply bow to these words—' God's will be done ; '
' Lead us not into temptation,' words needless,
Would God be—knowing weakness—so heedless ;
'Tis not by prayer selfish, sickening praise,
The Almighty to heaven mankind will raise ;
If to heaven mankind goes from earth at all,
Deeds must be done, we by these rise or fall ;
Blaspheme ye at places in the Prayer Book,
At prayers for weather, etcetera, look !
With intercessions for persons second,
Think ye prayers second-hand will be reckoned,
Prayers framed thus appear to show but just this,
God knows for best, not lets things go amiss ;
Prayer or no prayer, God's Will will be done,
And thus to Eternity will ever it run,
Quite incomprehensible though it be
Logically, or illogically."

Did he the Bible ever read ?
I asked. At first he took no heed
Of the question, but asked again,
Summed he that up in coolest vein—

" All heed pay to each good precept therein,
Good rejected, by Satan tended, is sin ;
But you may depend, had God written that book,
No one therein who searched would vainly look
For what he sought, whereas, strive as they may,
Therein can *some* find not enlightening ray
Of hope, that will bear literal translation,
Logically ; nought but botheration
Spiritual is there therein ; through and through
Doth it savour of the priest priestly, New
And Old alike God's ways to man's shaping.
Inconsistencies therein wide gaping
Pass over, and Moses' conjuring trick,
And Jacob, that revered rogue of rogues, quick ;
Just peep at David's songs wherein asks he
For what?   Blessings earthly ! more than heavenly !
And on enemies curses ! like a child
Peevish, by too indulgent parents spoiled ;

But ask the more important question—Why
The Book was written ?   To shew men how to die ?
Then what becomes of those who never heard
Of the Book, or of Christ one single word,
Giving Hell such preponderance of the Dead
As would have weighed Heaven down—feathers *versus* lead ?
And of those who have, yet cannot believe—
Whose powers of reason will not let deceive
Faith, which, 'tis said, shall be given to but few,
And those few chosen of the Lord ?   Think you
That the love, justice, of an Almighty God
Impartial ?   To reason's gift it seems most odd,
But soul saved, Bible-wise, what means it ?   Heaven gained ?
Granted !   But when there what has soul obtained ?
Riches in Heaven !   Pray of what do these consist ?
According to the Bible, a long list
Of all things earthly, stones precious, and gold,
Such as Heaven ethereal could not hold,
Of all things evil on this earth the root,
With God, earthly fashion, presiding, to boot
In raiment gorgeous, unnecessary,
On throne golden seated !   A Tale very
Well suited for the ages dark of the past,
But only to be shortly, with Fables old, cast,

As God's gift, Precious (increasing in light)
Reason, illumines superstitious night.
Oh ! how pitiful to hear ignorance say,
' I am one of the saved,' Philistine way
To their own defects blind, but whose desire
For life aggrandised heart setteth on fire,
Hugging themselves with the idea They, They,
And of their creed only, journey straightway.
But against that that makes happy not a breath,
With all creeds will it be the same at death,
Be there heaven or hell or neither at all,
Best done each for best may hope at the call.
'Tis not to those happy in Faith I speak,
To those whose Reason will not Faith let seek,
Who of God cannot ignore that best part,
Reason within, when war's Brain *versus* Heart ;
And—to warn of Parson inutility,
Working on Brain imbecility.
Trinity ignoring, that quicksand reef
Whereon whomsoe'er touches comes to grief,
Christ sent especially to save the Jews,
He whom that Nation repudiates, eschews,
Proof resting solely on a woman's word,
A newly-married virgin, aye absurd,

Exempting example setting for—what?

Thoughts vile and deeds I dare contemplate not,

Who, who can shameless in secret mind,

Christ's origin contemplate? can we find

Aught therein but Almighty degradation?

Of virtuous thought all spoilation?

To whom the wicked, dying, need but say,

'Lord, save me,' to have washed sins clean away;

Just heaven, a method so easy to reach,

Indulged would hell make on this earth for each;

For who in his dealings through life need care,

If to heaven from earth he thus easy went there.

Sacrificially though God can give and take,

Sacrifice to lesser greater cannot make;

Almighty though God be, even He, He,

Cannot destroy Form, but change Universally;

But could He, where lies the sacrifice? Trinity true,

Christ was, and is;—But flatly tell I you,

In the eyes of God an abomination,

'Tis but the Plot of the Priestly Nation,

Who uphold, and yea ever will uphold

All blindfold doctrines that return them gold,

Nor Book, nor can *that* intercession save,

Second-hand, on which Parsons earthy rave

And crave credulity—God's precious gift
Of Reason wrecking—though ever adrift
Goes reason quite, where Parsons are concerned,
To sentimentalists, they are so learned,
Any 'rot' believe these what Parsons say,
Thus have they had (and will) ever their way."

Again frantically
More so continued he.

"Parsons but work on the Sixth Sense,
Religion called, at man's expense ;
For man's soul they care not a jot,
They preach for How much can be got.
All prejudice itself are they,
Arrant impostors, Birds of Prey
(No, I do not mean spelt with an A).
Thus let me prove true what I say,
Howe'er they subject twist and twirl,
(For which poor sheep are shorn and bled,
Nor heaven guaranteed for that when dead.)
They can but set poor brains awhirl
They do but set poor brains awhirl

For who the future can unfurl?

Not they the future can unfurl!

But Death the future can unfurl!

And for that Death itself is doubtful.

(What Reason doth each mortal preach

A Parson can but only teach,

Hope! Hope! that dead, soul heaven may reach).

Thus than their's there is no calling

So useless. Hypocrisy, cant, bawling,

Form its stock in Trade, by which dishes

Save but they of loaves and fishes—

Save! Ha! beg, cadge, steal—"

Silence, man! Hold—-

But he went on fiercer full five-fold,

" Who but argue thus, Truth Truth is,

Like women argue, Because it is;

Who preach a doctrine so hollow

So diversified, cannot agree

Even their own fraternity

That Rationalism cannot follow;

Who —— 'em!"

I rushed from him ; would hear no more ;
From the cell bolted through the door,
For the moment horror-stricken quite ;
Yet soon thought struck me in this light—

Whilst Parsons themselves advertise
So modestly, who feels surprise
From Censure they be not exempt,
For self-praise who feels but contempt?

True Religion will always hide,
Like modest violet, all self-pride ;
And then, like lily, pure and white,
Will heavenly shine with God-iike light.

Richard, luckily, time was given,
To repent his views before quite driven
From this too wicked, envious world,
Ere, by man's law, to other hurled ;
Amongst rough prisoners was he placed,
With other miscreants sore disgraced.
And sent away beyond the seas,
Stern outraged justice to appease.

He cherished thought, Jane will be true;
Of Rattle's visits nothing knew,
Which cheered his heart in solitude,
Thus may the Proverb be construed—
"It is folly to be wise when
Sweet ignorance is bliss." Amen.
Next comes the wedding; so be it.
Of course, Richard did not see it.

PART XVII.

"Oh! That I had wings like a dove,
    Then would I flee away and be at rest,"
Oh! soothing words of heavenly love
    Where there, say they, Soul dwells for ever blest.

Heaven! Heaven! what means the magic word,
    So soothing! shall nought we there earthy find?
Can aught leave earth?   None ever heard,
    When there, shall we know friends—to earth be blind?

Could heaven to man be heaven without
    An earthy taint?   Can spirit itself free
Of body instinct?—Put to rout
    All thoughts of good, bad, past humanity?

"Oh ! that I had wings like a dove,
  Then would I flee away and be at rest,"
Can spirit rest ?—Here or above ?
  Never !—Then would oblivion be best ?

Ay ! Would oblivion be best ?
  I ask, but say not.   This bear well in mind,
With nought existing is there rest,
  Be it soul or matter of living kind ! !

      *   *   *   *

Last part reminds me of that list
I promised, which I yet have missed,
Where Parsons preach their very best,
Gratefully ! after six days' rest !
Business first, pleasure last,
The Wedding next, this chapter past.

As once remarked on second thoughts
(Which often make of first ones noughts)
Attempt I not where to send you,
Fear I a helping hand to lend you,

Lest parsons might come down on me
With Sectarian Trade Jealousy.

No.　On third thoughts, will I steer clear
Of subjects such—Mrs. G—— I fear—
And simply substitute instead,
What Captain Richard Glover said,
When visiting him once before,
I rushed with horror through cell door.

" At True Religion—mark me well,
I scoff not, only do I tell,
Or speak, of what seems out of place,
Which all Religions doth disgrace.
Please do not call me Atheist !
Non-Religious ! because a list
Of follies seem to cross my sight ;
I may but see in but wrong light ;
Bigotry I hate, pretend *I* not
To perfection minus a blot ;
Nor do I point in disrespect
At Doctrines of Combative Sect
(Combative to a shadow, aye,
Each swears its own the only way);

But short life prompts—I must here mention,
That which calls forth laughable attention.

Go where you will, to High Church, Low,
To Chapel, chimneyless, or no,
(T'is self must settle where to go);
But most careful be lest you mistake,
Chapel for Church, if for church you make,
To find, too late, you have been sold
By Brave Dissenting Builders Bold,
Who Chapels like Church now so gild,
With exterior of a churchly build,
That savors of Dissenting Trap,
To catch some Ritualistic Chap,
Who may be to the Town a Stranger,
From might be Ritualistic* Danger.
Which calls forth laughable attention,
From some Sects I need not mention,
Oh ! dear me, no.

—

* Had he lived in the present days,
What would he have said of the ways
Of lawless Ritualism now,
Hatcham, to wit, with its Sunday row.

No business of mine ?   Quite right !

Then look we now at, by the light

Of Dissent, Rank Ritualism,

From Mother Church, the Devil's Schism.*

Dissent nor True Church like it not,

Call Ritualism much to hot.

Idolatry, with the bow and bend,

Though from what worse is heaven defend,

(But God but knows where will it end.)

The Priest in absolution they

Will introduce, say yea, not Nay,

* IIe also said—
                Unitarianism
Seems to be the more rational road
To Heaven, of but One God the abode,
And one only, there cannot be more,
Perplexed supremacy would reign sore ;
Even Supreme Omnipotence would fade,
Did, or had God, ever called in aid ?
Sad thought ! but there is full quite as much
Idolatry in Ceremonies such
As Christians practise, to say the least,
As with Heathens taught by Heathen Priest.
Ah ! with what worldly glasses paint we
God—On earth that for ever to be
Mystery.

Private Confession and—what next?
Illustrated by Scripture text,
That both are right and in accord
With truthful rendering of the Word.

Calling forth laughable attention
From some sects I need not mention.
Oh! dear me, no.

No business of mine, do you say?
This time, Yes, though short be my stay
In this world; and of yours this way—
Taxes must we pay to the State,
For what we like not, pay tithe-rate;
Let Parsons fantastically play
As they please with the cash we pay.
The Church, by means of taxation,
Belongs to each man in the nation;
And Parsons have no right to change
Ceremony, introduce strange,
Or with Popery co-arrange,
Whilst one farthing they get of State pay,
Then with what is disliked do away.

Now calling forth loud lamentation
To Free England degradation.
Oh! dear me, yes.

But what *is* State Church in this, our land ?
Like all sorts, a varied mixed band,
Where State Rules Nil is seen nor heard,
Where livings ever are transferred
To highest bidders, few well fit
To guide flocks who them under sit ;
Not but that those best point the way
Who have themselves oft gone astray
(Had Solomon never gone wrong,
Could he have advised thus strong ?)
But Livings are a speculation
In this our civilised nation.
A Disgrace, lamentable sore.
Now for a few adverse sects more—"

" Hold," I said, " than these too many,
Better would Heaven be reached without any
Than where they all so disagree
In Sectarian Jealousy."

" But let us quiz " (on would he go)

"And ask what is " (though said I no).

" *Sectarianism ?* " Speculation,

Parsons Preying on Creation ;

Established Habit, by Priests named

Religion—But mark ! Mind can be framed ;

Habit doth by long Custom grow

To anything ; thus Religion's show,

Abetted by Legislature,

Long ages taking to mature,

Has now become *Second Nature.*

But its true nomenclature

Is Worshipful Gesticulation,

(Ever changing with the Fashion

To suit the age—the Sister Passion)

Spiced by Sixth Sense Inclination—

Result, Spiritual Botheration ;

And Fashion means, Abroad at home,

Wheree'er we be,

Conformity,

" At Rome we all must do like Rome ;"

Lest Mrs. Grundy, over the way,

And neighbours kind, might something say,

If to the House of God we went not,

To Sectarianism bent not,

To fatten fat Priests spent not ;

House of God! Forsooth! a place where

Fashions Congregate, a Priestly Snare,

Where lawless Priests do all they dare,

Where rival fashions proudly stare,

And wealth is favoured—Oh! Beware,

Ye thoughtless! Think, when go ye there,

Where Bitter Bigotry reigns odd,

Can This House be The House of God?

House of God ? which lightning smites as well

As Satan's so-called Prince of Hell.

(Say Sub-King, Subject to a Greater,

If existing (?), His Creator,

Who, as of all, its Dictator,

Emperor of Hell must, must be

As Supreme Omniscient Almighty ;

Or Permits God Hell to run riot ?

Or Sentence mild Satan defy it ?

If to foul hell God ever sends ?

No!!! To Heaven God's sentence ever tends.)

Yea! Nor Priest, nor Church, Future, Past,

Howe'er our lot in life be cast,

God will arrange life right at last.

What is to be will surely be,

Nothing can alter God's Decree ;

God made, and must provide end for,

Regardless of all Ancient Law

And Priestly interpretation,

Frightening, by way of damnation,

To Ceremonies barbarous ;

God will in Heaven Harbour us

Without such absurdities.   Away,

Then, with all tomfoolery, pray,

(For divers creeds but go to shew,

None Nothing of the Future know.)

All that we have on earth to do

Is ' *As we would be done unto* '

Expressing love for God *deeds* through ;   ·

God wants no more, This is man's best ;

To His Loving Mercy leave the rest ;

If but to these rules man adheres,

Man never need have Future Fears ;

Then Heathens, Christians, All will He save,

Or Curses God part life He gave."

PART XVIII.

"Fish you with a hairline and fly?"

"Artistically not," says I,

"What catch you?" Astonished, says he:

"On the hook, whatever may be,

Provided nought breaks, never doubt,

One pulls in or the other out."

Ha! Fishing defined by Rule of Three,

After Doctor Johnson, I see;

He, no wonder, never fish caught,

Pot-hunter, they knew him, and shy fought.

Ay! but it is a cruel sport,

And but for that I should have nought

So weak writ.

A live worm take (what fun),

From end to end through its body run

A barbed hook. Throw it in the stream,

Watch. Whilst indulging daylight dream

Let the poor worm fiend-tortured die
In unutterable agony.
Heaven pitying, then mark the float
Move, indicating down the throat
Of some poor fish the hook has gone,
Together with the worm thereon.
Now strike hard, that the barb may stick
Fast in the fish's gullet quick ;
If heavy, then, play it—fine sport,
That is, tear the fish's throat till caught.
If a small one has been landed,
Worm-baiting may be then disbanded
Run a needle through from head to tail
Threaded with a hook, then let trail
The fish on that (how long 'twill live
Is wonderful, but do not give
Heed or thought) ; then hope some Jack
May down his throat the morsel snack.
The best of live bait is the frog,
Has more vitality—lucky dog (?)
Tortured it may be many ways,
One of the Fine Arts now-a-days
Is Fishing—called The Gentle Art,

Gentle, very, on the Fisher's part,
Pity Fishers ne'er felt the smart.

  *   *   *   *

Now to sweet Cupid's fishing-ground,
A place where souls are hooked and bound
With tackle endless wily wound.

  Organ-pipes pealing,
  Rising from kneeling,
  Voices male stealing,
   Soft dying in echoes above ,
  Heaven below seeming,
  Mind setting dreaming
  Thought filling teeming
   Of life new when dead, and God's love.

  Yet a void leaving,
  A sort of deceiving,
  For something more grieving,
   Like half-finished broken off tale ;
  But for this, divine,
  The drawing the line,
  To Music confine
   Male voices without sweet female.

Well comprehended,
Both voices blended
Thus God intended,
    Of sexes conjointly should be ;
Organists clever,
Make up for never,
Deficiency ever,
    Voice female from choir harmony.

Thus mark ye through life,
Midst trials too rife,
It softens world's strife,
    God meant not exclude women here ;—
Meant sexes should mingle,
Never keep single,
Hearts with love tingle
    Meant all should a partner take dear.

At St. George's, Hanover Square,
Were Rattle and Jane married there,
And did not the on-lookers stare,
For it was a most stylish affair,

P

With whitest of horses three pair,
For Bride and Bridegroom, I swear,
Postilions in white powdered hair,
Sweet bridesmaids selected with care,
(For Bridesmen a dangerous snare),
A Regiment there was, I declare,
Enough, and some over, to spare,
The Bride to support and up bear
The trial which most women dare
The world over everywhere.

In the time of Adam and Eve
They made not such fuss, I believe,
Nor Bridesmaids nor Parson had they
To witness the Bride given away ;
But, wishing none now to deceive,
That in marriage neither doth grieve,
As witnesses bring we our friends,
And solemnly courting thus ends.

Quite funny felt Jane on that day
Appointed to give hand away ;

Did her thoughts, I wonder, run wild
To Over the Seas and—hush, child,
Pasts forget, to the altar go,
Where Brides ought not, if thoughts stray so.

Brave Bridesmen were there to support
Timid Bridegroom as Bridesmen ought ;
Several Parsons were there, of course,
One possessed not sufficient force
To fashionably tie the knot tight,
One now looks ridiculous quite :
The organist played, whilst his clerk
Hard pumped in the wind from the dark ;
The organ loud growled, gave a squeak,
Stopped—Head Parson was then heard to speak—

" Who taketh this woman for wife ? "
" I do, for the rest of my life,"
Said Rattle, "to love and to cherish
Until she, or I, or both perish."
Then, turning to Jane, Parson said,
Dubiously shaking his head,
" Woman, wilt thou in deed, thought, word,
Obey this man ? "

(Question absurd
To ask a woman thus to do,
But marriage makes an one of two,
Which accounts for the after bliss
Of wedded life, Connubial Kiss.)

" I will," the youthful timid bride,
In softest accents thus replied,
But mentally added "not" thereto,
Silently vowing never thus do,
Woman-like all over, but there,
Softly coax, Tiffs soon round square.

" I will," in turn, growled bridegroom slower,
Gravely, in an octave lower,
When quick began the organ blower ;
For the knot was tied, the job was done,
Siamese Twin-like, two now were one.

Next to the vestry all adjourned,
Paid the fees that had been earned,
(Which first man did to all concerned,
Yet still for more officials yearned,)

Whilst in arm chair the Bride sat seated
By crowding Bridesmaids over-heated,
Who, the bride in trying to support,
Did not their duty as they ought,
But in frenzied zeal a bottle must
Of smelling salts up her nose thrust.
Poor thing, it was an awful trial,
Even Rattle wished he had a phial
Of spirits undiluted, raw,
He felt so downy in the jaw.

But when the Wedding March was heard—
   Which spinsters shelved, oh! hate to hear,
   Sour grapes to them, makes feel quite queer—
Each soul with freshened spirit stirrred;
All from the vestry quickly cleared,
Walked to the door and there were cheered
By all the urchins of the street,
Who thought the sight a jolly treat;
All in their carriages then get,
A merry, laughing, chaffing set,
And take a drive, after that meet
To partake of wedding breakfast treat

Of choicest things, superbly cooked,
And very nice each dainty looked,
On Standard Silver, Virgin Gold,
A fortune quite, were value told ;
Then came speeches and good wishes,
When they had cleared away some dishes,
That Bride might better cut the cake
Which took a thousand men to make.
The happy couple then soon left,
Thus did the guests of them bereft,
One by one until there were
Remaining but that Jovial Pair,
The Parson and Doctor, who each spoke
Of marriage as a standing joke,
Each other rallied on the spoil
Resulting from a Maiden's Coil.

" I have had mine, yours is to come,"
The Parson said ! Said Doctor Rum,
" Remember there is yet in store,
For you rich fees for Christenings more ;
But, I give credit, you get cash,
You never risk a Bankrupt's Smash,

Ha! Lucky dog, ha! ha!" both laughed,
And thus the two on Weddings chaffed.

The Happy Pair travelling alone,
The Bride indulged a little moan
Of affected grief, secret joy,
That she had got her darling boy
Securely bound, tied, wedded fast;
Then as they steamed the stations past,
(Dreams realized of joy at last)
They ' Kissey-kissey'd ' in the Carriage,
Congratulations on their marriage.
Arrived late at their journey's end,
The Bride was glad to footsteps bend
Upstairs, disrobed, but left the light
Full burning for her husband bright,
Who, soon to bed after wended,
Said ' Good Night' just as day ended :
Yes, twelve o'clock that moment struck,
Ah ! happy couple, wish them luck.

PART XIX.

Bridesmaids! Could the wide world wheel without them?
Bless the darlings! there is that about them
Sets the sterner heart all in a flutter,
Whisperings soft wish tongue attempt to utter.

Oh! Like Richmond Maids of Honor, were
They as comeatable, dark and fair;
Maids there perfection quite attain,
There, Maids distinguished highly reign,
Agreeable ever,
Too crusty, never.
Daintily supreme.   Haughty? Nay!
Nor ever want they their own way,
Oh (seven for Six-pence is their price)
Richmond Bachelor's Paradise.

Maids of Honor, what thoughts upspring
At the words, associations bring
Back of the past, when ladies then—
Hale, hardworking, non-presuming
Princess style-like non-assuming—
Industrious help-mates were of men.
Exclaims the Modern Modeste, " Ah !
Comparisons are odious, bah !
Women the same were always—Men
I grant you were deserving then,
Brave, Courteous, Gallant, young and old
Now seek they wives but for their gold."
Madam, Mis-take me not, I pray,
(When I a widower am you may)
Equally have ladies' just claim
To all that is worthy the name
Now as of yore,
I meant so before
And nothing more ;
Kindly Pardon mind wandering,
Useless thoughts of the past pondering,
But without more words squandering

Let me explain,

Why there they reign

As ask you, Supreme.   Made of many

Ingredients, price One Penny,

Renowned, though local, wide and far,

These Richmond Maids of Honor are,

A sort of Cheese Cake, par-tic-u-lar ;

Extra at the Star and Garter nice

Though somewhat higher there the price.*

＊   ＊   ＊   ＊   ＊

They say " One Wedding makes many ! "

Without " One " could there be any?

Stupid ! of course not—Certainly—No.

Stupid ? no more than the phrase so ;

True, but nine-tenths of these old saws

Are—What ? but Idiotic bores,

Which would-be wise conceit assumes

Depth of knowledge thereon presumes.

---

* Breakfasting at Richmond on a certain memorable occasion, I was exceedingly surprised to find figuring on ¦the Menu, Maids of Honor. I indulged in a few. But, the above eruption was the consequence.

On the Altar Rail Cupid sat
At Jane's Wedding, looking thereat
Intently, though of course, unseen,
Nor has there ever wedding been
Where Cupid was not—looking out
For fresh victims. All round about
His aide-de-camp and staff were there
Hovering (unseen of course) in air,
Watching the Bridesmaids' winning looks
At Bridesmen cast instead of books.

Venus was there, Pensive and Sad,
At the finish she seemed more glad,
Yet she departed softly crying
With bosom heaving deeply sighing
As women do at weddings oft ;
A woman's heart, oh ! is so soft !

Lest Cupid should fair heart annoy,
(He is a most mischievous boy)
Venus aids him, gives direction,
(Women on love are circumspection)
And Cupid's bow is useless bent
If Venus gives not her consent.

No sooner did the church door close
On the Verger, than there loud arose
A joyous shout, and to dancing
Set Cupid's staff lively prancing.

One went up in the organ loft
Played fantasias, loud and soft,
Of Bononcini, Bach, Beethoven,
Balfe, Lizst, Wagner, interwoven,
(No musical medley hotch-potch
Mind, but master-pieces minus scotch)
As they should be to perfection
To a fairy's beat direction.

When all had danced themselves half-wild
Cupid appeared; that Godly child
(Perched himself on an organ pipe)
With cheeks like cherries when full ripe,
And Chubby limbs, quite a model,
A little child who just could toddle,
But with fully-fledged wings a pair
That swiftly, softly, cleft the air,

When on love errand bent—a Child
A naked little boy who wild
Sets the fairer sexes raving,
For sweethearts sets all girls a craving,

Suddendly church fittings self changed
Into Drawing-room well arranged
As if by magic without noise;
Then were seen other little boys
Like Cupid dressed (quite naked stark
Style fashionable with Nations dark),
Winged only, but with small darts armed
No bow—Cupid's Infantry charmed
Preliminary ticklers were these
Who first were sent to soften, please
The maiden heart it to prepare,
For Cupid's dart to be sent there.

Trumpet calls now did loudly broach
The Goddess Venus, her approach,
Who, in killing robes, now appeared,
(Fashions latest—cherubs cheered)

Then came her retinue of beauties,

(Venus assisting in her duties)

Whom she sends flirting to perplex,

In dreams, hearts of the sterner sex,

Who maketh love o'er hearts to steal,

When Venus gives the coup-d'œil—

I should have said the coup-de-grâce,

Makes lads for lasses " ask mamma."

When all were seated, Venus said—

" Cupid Advise—Who ought be led

To the altar next ?   Which Bridesmaid

Of to-day would be afraid

To wed, think you ? "

            " Your charming grace

Doth doth, methinks, your words misplace.

Not one, you know, would be afraid

To be to Matron changed from Maid—

Love girls to be left on the shelf ? "

" Hush, Cupid! let each girl speak for self ;

Think not girls desire to marry !

'Tis horrid men won't let them tarry

Single—Pshaw !—

Now tell me.—Hark! hear!
Some one on entrance bent, I fear."

'Twas the Sexton come to toll the bell,
A funeral monotonous knell,
All precipitately fled pell-mell.

Plans thwarted! or there would have been
Bridesmaids to Bridesmen married clean;
Another would each one have gained,
Yet "one and one" would have remained,
No more! ay! less! but half an one!
For when the marriage deed is done,
Arithmetical nomenclature
Reigns paradoxical in nature;
Or, in other phraseology,
By means of etymology,
Thus shewing our philology,
With to married an apology,
Addition becomes division!
Call we it—but not in derision—
"Sweet Cupidiacal elision."

PART XX.

—o◯o—

Hear Morning Bells ringing,
Singing, gaily singing
   In gleeful strife,
Of wedded Youth, Beauty,
Duty, Love, Love, Duty,
'Twixt man and wife.

List! Evening Bells pealing,
Stealing, music stealing,
   O'er hill and dale,
O'er green meadows swelling.
Telling, softly telling
   Many a Tale.

     ✳   ✳   ✳   ✳   ✳

Marriage, like Law, is Lottery sore,
Than the first case few wish for more ;
Body marries Body, but Mind—Mind
Not once in a thousand will you find ;
But when unite both nought goes amiss,
Experienced then is earthly bliss.

With her beloved darling, Cappy—
   For such she called the Captain Brave,
   For which a kiss he then her gave—
Was Jane always after happy ?

No ! No ! a thousand times No ! No !
What is more, it is mostly so
With unequal matches.—Never
Will happiness last for ever.
Even with best-assorted (Married) pair,
Not reigns all happiness always there.
Honey always both are not.—A Row
Is sure to crop up sometimes somehow ;
Ay ! Life would be insipid, no doubt,
Minus sweet fallings in and out ;

All happiness was never meant
To earthly mortals to be sent,
For then to leave this world would be
A Trial Sore of misery.

Jane had been sent abroad and taught
Everything Titled ladies ought.
Naturally clever and quick,
And helped by every Master's Trick,
In the art of learning, teaching,
She was not very long reaching
Ordinary perfection, but then,
She never with the Upper Ten
Of Titled Ladies felt at ease,
Blood bred they plebian seemed to frieze.
She tried her best her lord to please
By carefully avoiding mention
Of her parents, strict attention
To which was specially required,
Though oft to see them she desired.

Poor creatures! Losing their daughter,
They felt like fish out of water;

It preyed so much upon their mind
That each with each sad fault did find
At consent given to the match,
Though both then thought it was Grand Catch.

About the Captain.   How felt he ?
Well, with men it is differently ;
Men, as a rule, above their station
May marry ;   Men's occupation
(Married) is to superintend
Money matters, with which they blend
Pleasure, which slyly call they work,
Though underneath there oft doth lurk
Deeds wives know not of.
                                        Did he love
His little low-born turtle dove ?
At least never had she ought of,
(He of her so ever thought of)
To complain.   All heart could desire,
She had except her loving sire
And mother, for whom she secret wept,
But to herself the secret kept.

Yet, could she have asked her parents there,
Would she have done so?

                No, she dare
Not even to herself it own,
She, with her rise, had proudly grown;
Of lowly birth was now ashamed,
As if for that she ought be blamed.

Now there are lots of sorts of pride,
Some worthy, others we deride
Most deservedly so, but of all
None doth deserve so loud a call
Of censure, as wish to disown
Honest Parents when we have grown
Advanced in the social scramble,
Whilst parent stock remains a bramble.
It is not vulgar thus applied,
Deserves worse name does such a pride;
But there is a Pride called Stinking,
This must be it I am thinking.
(Oh! stiff-necked stuck-up stinking pride,
Ye owners thereof, blush and hide,
Ye but self-murder stab, deride,
To Hell thereby unwitting glide.)

Jane tried to drive her's from her mind
By sending presents of all kind,
At sight of which their old hearts bled,
For Jane, to them, was of the dead.
They could not see her but to cheer
Their broken hearts, talked of their dear,
Still dear, dear daughter, but the tear
Would trickle down at hallowed name,
Still loved the same, yet not the same,
That once she was when all were poor,
Ere Jane's skeleton barred the door
Repining almost drove them wild,
They wanted so to see their child,
To own whom Jane's proud pride forbade,
" God bless her though," they daily said.,
" God bless her though," they nightly prayed,

Live skeletons there are we know,
Yet dead ones live and larger grow,
Skeletons in each house are there
And Jane's was this we have laid bare ;

Skeletons differ in degree,
Quality and intensity ;
But that which all must most deride
Is Skeleton of Stinking Pride.
With such none can be happy here,
Nor those who own not parents dear ;
If both are honest, why feel ashamed
To hear them in your presence named,
Think not your parents you disgrace
Should you be raised to higher place ;
Nor what they were exaggerate,
A fashion prevalent of late,
Position never makes mind great !

Poor Friends too we need not disown,
Honest Poverty never was known
To be a sin.—Then forbidden
Stinking Pride in hearts be hidden,
Than which there are few sins much worse ;
Yet it forms the Skeleton Curse
Of Society, and will ever,
Eradicate it shall we never,
For it is part of—though it be
Despicable—Human Frailty.

Having finished—Fare thee well—

Some Lady asks, "His wedding day
Did Rattle repent?" I must not say :
Tell I you this—judge as you may—

Jane practised not *That Highest Art,*
Most charming on a woman's part.
(Men want humouring, or they smart)
One's self-agreeable the making—
Ye married therein be painstaking—
And though the term some may stagger,
She was what is termed a nagger.

Oh ! oh ! a thousand voices cry,
Whilst hands of whitest upward fly.
Of course he was not happy ?
                    Well,
As I said before, I must not tell.

Farewell once more, I hope we may,
Dear Reader, meet another day ;

If you these lines appreciate,
Another Tale I will create.
Or, or, continue the tale thus :—
Let Jane (dispensing with the fuss)
Introduce a sweet cherub boy,
Girls' hearts expressly to annoy ;
Then somebody else—a girl—to play,
(Serve him right) with his heart as she may,
Serious subjects diminish
On Love Commence, on Love FINISH.

www.ingramcontent.com/pod-product-compliance
Lightning Source LLC
Chambersburg PA
CBHW030312270326
41926CB00010B/1331